A Positive Way Couple's Guide

Talk to Me

How to Create Positive Loving Communication

by

Steven & Catherine Martin

The Positive Way™

Positive Publishing
Williamsville, New York

Published by Positive Publishing
123 E. Pinelake Drive, Williamsville, NY 14221

ISBN: 0-9659328-0-X

Manufactured in the United States of America

Library of Congress Cataloging Number: 97-92268

ATTENTION RELATIONSHIP COLLEAGUES: Quantity discounts are available on bulk purchases of this book for training or counseling purposes.

The Positive Way™ conducts seminars and work-shops on a variety of relationship topics including communication. See pages 150 & 151 for summaries.

**For information contact:
The Positive Way, 123 E. Pinelake Drive
Williamsville, NY 14221
phone 716-639-0225 • 800-664-4773**

This edition is printed on acid-free paper that meets the American National Standards Institute Z39.48 Standard.

Talk to Me

Silence, lonely silence,
creeps like ivy,
poison ivy,
through the garden
of my heart.
My heart
it aches.
I cry for you
to talk to me.

How well you communicate through both the bad and
good times determines the ultimate health of your
relationships. Relationships flourish or wither
depending on what you say and how you say it.

Dedication

We dedicate this book to lovers.
Lovers who are creating new love in real life
one word at a time.

The Positive Way Mission

Our mission is to educate, enlighten and inspire personal growth
in a positive way.

Acknowledgments

We thank our families, friends and all of our other teachers along this journey of life and love. Their support, each in its own way, has nurtured our growth and helped us create *The Positive Way*.

Our many clients and students shared their lives with us as we shared with them. It is their stories that are woven together into the pages of this book. We have planted many flowers and pulled many weeds together.

We are grateful to our editors Karen Marie Kauderer and Susan Blackley of *Written Image* who helped us breathe clarity and love into these words.

Thank you to David Jarzab the very talented artist who created the book cover and logo design.

CONTENTS

About the Authors

Catherine and I have talked our way through many problems in our lives and share a love that grows stronger and stronger each day. We learned a lot about love before we married, each for the second time. We have learned even more in the fourteen years since then, as we've practiced and taught the art of loving and the art of positive, loving communication. Our extensive research and personal experience has shown that the creation of positive, loving communication is critical to the vitality of any type of love.

We are now sharing our commitment to love with the rest of the world through our seminars, books and private consultations. We have written this book to help you create the loving relationships that you seek. Thank you for allowing us to share our thoughts and experiences with you through the words of this book. May your love flourish like a beautiful flower garden.

Introduction

We invite you to enrich your loving relationships with *Talk to Me*. **We will help you discover new ways to create the love you want in your life one word at a time.**

You are human, with fears, desires, needs, wants, expectations and strong emotions that you don't always understand. At the same time you've chosen to share your life with your partner. Now you have your own emotions as well as his/hers to share. This isn't always easy, especially with all the pressures and expectations of life. It is sad that communication is usually the first thing that breaks down in a loving relationship. When you need each other the most, you are heading in different directions, unable to talk with each other. You can change that. **You can come back together by learning to communicate in a positive way. This book will help show you the way.**

Relationships do not *live* in silence.

Communicating is much easier and safer when you have a process and guidelines to follow. *Talk to Me* will teach you many techniques, including the important Couple's Fair Exchange Process, which has three straightforward and powerful elements: 1) Equal time for each to speak, 2) A commitment to reach understanding before making a decision, and 3) Four guidelines for communicating based on understanding, kindness, honesty and respect. The Couple's Fair Exchange Process is both a guide and a safety net for even the most troubled relationships.

Talk to Me gives you clear examples to follow in order to create the positive change you want in your life.

A relationship may be likened to a garden. You reap what you sow and success or failure depends on how well you tend it. Words from the heart presented in a positive way have the chance of taking root and growing like flowers into the garden of a balanced intimate relationship. One kind word or deed can go a very long way. Negative words or deeds, like weeds, can cause considerable damage. With enough damage, the garden goes to ruin and soon only bitter weeds will grow – in silence.

Talk to Me begins with a story of a newlywed couple, Peter and Anne, whose relationship is already in trouble after less than a year together. Their relationship is like a garden that is full of weeds of negative words and deeds, and more thorns are exchanged than the flowers of positive, loving communication. Let's follow their lives for a while and listen to what is really going on.

Chapter One : Anne and Peter - A Story of a Loving Garden

Anne: "Peter, I could use some help with dinner. Couldn't you read the paper later? You spend more time with your friends than with me." (thinking: I'm tired and I miss him. It's been a long day at the office. I bet he's tired, too. Why won't he come and at least talk to me? I'm lonely.)

Peter: "Hey, I'm beat. Just give me a break for a minute." (thinking: Rough day and bad weather, too. Anne's been bugging me about spending time with the guys instead of her. I don't understand. Why won't she just get off my back? I'm frustrated.)

Anne annoyed: "Do you want dinner or not?" (thinking: I thought this was a partnership but it sure doesn't feel like one right now.)

Peter heading for the door: "Look, I don't care. If it's that much trouble, I'll just go get something at the bar." (thinking: She asks me to be sure to be home for dinner and then makes a big deal out of a few minutes rest. I wish I could understand what she wants. I'm just too tired and frustrated to deal with this now.)

Door slams. Anne heads to the bedroom in tears. (thinking: What did I do wrong? We can't even talk. Why doesn't he love me any more?)

Peter driving to the bar upset. (thinking: What did I do wrong? We just can't ever talk. Doesn't she love me?)

The next day at work Anne is talking to her friend Mary over coffee.

Anne: "You know, Mary, I'm not sure it's going to work out. Peter and I haven't been married very long now and we just seem to be moving farther and farther apart. I think he loves me and I think I still love him but it just doesn't feel the same. We never talk anymore. We only seem to fight and I'm not even sure what about."

Mary: "I know what you mean. Frank and I were headed that way and six months ago I'd have bet on a divorce. I know what they say about hurting the kids and all, but I figured it might be better to separate rather than to just teach the kids how to fight and pout."

Anne: "I watched you and Frank at the company party last month and you two looked like newlyweds. What happened, a miracle?"

Mary: "Well, yes and no. It was really more like waking up slowly to a new day, after working hard in the garden."

Anne: "Wait, you've lost me. What's this about waking up slowly and gardens. You live in an apartment and I know you can be grumpy before your second cup of coffee."

Mary: "If you think about your relationship with yourself and others as a garden, negative thoughts as weeds and positive thoughts as flowers, you'll begin to see what I'm saying. Every time Frank and I argued, we were spreading weeds in the garden."

Anne: "You mean our minds are like gardens, and thoughts and words can be like flowers or weeds?"

Mary: "Yes, that's it. My thoughts were full of the weeds of negativity and I just couldn't let my love blossom any more. Frank felt the same way. We just didn't talk about it or about much of anything. I don't know how we got there. I guess it just happened. We *let* it happen."

Anne: "So now what? How does that make a difference? I think I'd just feel worse if I realized what I've been doing wrong."

Mary: "That's true. I did feel worse for a while but I started practicing what I learned reading a book about positive, loving relationships and I changed my life. I started pulling some old dead weeds out of my garden. I even planted some flowers. I gave our neighbors some things they needed, but couldn't afford. I called my friend, Jane whom I hadn't spoken to in years. I began to feel better about myself and about Frank."

Anne: "I noticed you've been happier lately. I'm jealous."

Mary: "Anne, don't be jealous, that's a weed."

Anne: "Oh, I'm sorry. I really am happy for you."

Mary: "Thanks. I appreciate your kind thoughts."

Anne: "Did I just plant a flower?"

Mary: "Oh yes, and it's beautiful. Let's both enjoy it."

Anne: "I feel good. Thanks for talking with me. Can we continue at lunch tomorrow?"

Mary: "Yes. Now let's have a great afternoon."

Anne: "Thanks, Mary, I think we will."

3

Anne at home after work: "Hi, Peter, I'm home. Look, I'm sorry I got upset with you last night. I was just lonely and I guess I took it out on you." (truth)

Peter: " Yeah that's for sure. Does that mean you're going to try to talk me out of playing ball with the guys tonight?" (thinking: What's she looking for? I blew my stack too and yet she's apologizing. She must want something.) "What do you expect from me? You want me to stay home and not have friends." (thinking: I don't want to be here lonely with you. We have nothing to talk about.)

Anne: "Peter, I don't expect anything from you." (thinking: I've learned that if I give and give, I get nothing back.) "I don't want to argue, I just want you to have a good time at the game." (thinking: I hope you'll feel better about yourself and us.)

Peter: "Uh, well, okay. I might be late." (thinking: I feel good with the team. I trust them.)

At lunch with Mary the next day.

Mary: "Well, Anne, how did it go last night.?"

Anne: "I'm not sure but I think okay. We didn't fight but we didn't see much of each other either. I had the evening to myself. I just thought about what you said yesterday. I went to bed late and slept so peacefully, I didn't even hear Peter when he got home from the game."

Mary: "Did you plant any flowers?"

4

Anne: "I tried but I'm not sure Peter's ready. He came home later than usual. Come to think about it though, he did kiss me goodbye this morning. He doesn't do that much anymore. Maybe it was just because his team won the game. They're in fourth place now. I'd love to hear more about what you learned at the seminar but I've got to get back to work early. (thinking: I have a chance for the new manager's slot but the competition is rough. We may even be opponents.)

Mary: "What are you working on? Maybe I can help."

Anne: "Well, it's the Jones' project. I'm not sure you can help me." (thinking: Can I trust you?)

Mary: "Anne, I know the Jones' project well. I worked on that account last year before I changed departments. Please let me help you."

Anne: "Okay, thanks." (thinking: I hope I can trust her.)

Mary: "Oh, by the way try some more flowers with Peter. It always works with me when Frank does it. Let's get to work. I know we can do a great job for your boss."

At home that night:

Anne: "Peter, how was your game last night? It must have been a late one. I didn't even hear you come home."

Peter: "Look don't get on me about being late, okay? It went into overtime and then we had a couple of beers to celebrate." (thinking: There she goes again about my being with the guys. She just doesn't understand me.)

Anne: "Peter, there's no need to be annoyed. I'm really happy that you won and that you had a good time."

5

Peter: "You are?"

Anne: "Yes, let's go to Ronzoni's and get some pizza to celebrate."

Peter: "Yeah, that'd be nice. We haven't been there since we dated." (thinking: I wonder what she wants.)

At Ronzoni's:

Peter: "How's work? You haven't told me much about it in months." (thinking: Maybe if we talk about her she won't bug me.)

Anne: "Thanks for asking. It's really going well. Mary has been helping me a lot on the Jones' project and if I do well maybe I'll get that promotion."

Peter: "Wait a minute. Why trust her? I thought that Mary was up for that promotion too. Why would she help you? Maybe she's going to mess it up somehow or take all the credit."

Anne: "I thought a lot about that and even asked her why she was helping me. She said that there was enough success for everyone if we just shared it. Mary told me that she had enough confidence in herself that she could help me and we'd both win."

Peter: "How can that happen? How can you both win? (thinking: I don't believe it.) You'd better be careful. I like Mary and Frank, but something's going on here."

Anne: "Mary told me that she believed that the bosses would see what was going on. That they'd recognize our hard work and reward us both. She said that she'd be happy for me if I got

6

the promotion. There's plenty of opportunity for those who think positively. I don't think I understand everything she's telling me but I'm sure of one thing: I trust her. Don't you trust people any more? You used to say that trust was very important to you."

Peter: "Yes, I do. I trust my friends but you know, I think I trust you more than anyone. Just talking about it reminds me that it was trust in you that attracted me to you in the first place. Anyway, let me know what happens. You know we really could use the extra money from a raise. Besides Mary and Frank seem to have plenty of cash these days. Mary may not need the promotion as much as we do, but I think she's pretty competitive. Enough of that. How about some more of this good bread?"

Anne: "Thanks, Peter, it's so good to hear you say that about me. How are things at your work?"

Peter: "Anne, I really don't want to talk about it. Smith is kissing up to the boss again and it's a real pain." (thinking: I'm scared. My work isn't as good as Smith's but I just can't seem to find enough time to get everything done. There are rumors about a layoff and maybe I'll be the first to go.)

Anne: "I'd really like to talk about it. What's going on?" (thinking: I can sense something is wrong here but I don't know what. I'm getting worried.)

Peter: "Let's just drop it. It's not worth talking about." (thinking: I wonder if she'll divorce me if I lose my job. It could be the straw that breaks the camel's back.)

Anne: "Okay, I'm ready to go home." (thinking: What now? Where are the flowers in these weeds? Maybe Mary is wrong about all this stuff. All I see now is new weeds. Now Peter is worried about something at work that I didn't even know about before.)

Some days later at Anne's work, in the hall:

Mary: "Anne, where have you been? I was looking for you at lunch yesterday and you haven't returned my voice mail messages."

Anne: "I've been busy. You know, working on the Jones' project." (thinking: Yes, I avoided you yesterday. I was upset by what Peter had to say. Maybe I can't trust you on this crazy positive stuff. I just don't know.)

Mary: "I see you're worried. Maybe you've taken on too much too soon. I think it takes time to grow. If we expect too much too soon, when we're not ready, we can be disappointed. Please have lunch with me. We'll just talk about the weather. I promise. Okay?"

Anne: "Okay, but just the weather."

Mary: "Isn't the sky lovely?"

Anne: "Looks dark to me. I'm tired of the rain."

Mary: "I know what you mean but the water will make our gardens grow as long as there's not too much. Look at the sky again."

Anne: "Well, all I see is a bunch of clouds and some of them are raining pretty hard. I hope my car window doesn't leak again. That thing is such a junker. I wish I had a nice new one like you. Oh, I'm sorry. There I go again. Weeds, right?"

Mary: "Right. If you plant weeds that's all you'll get is weeds. Every negative thought becomes a negative thing. Pretty soon we're surrounded by negative things and we can't see our way out of the weeds. Now look at the sky again. Look at that shaft of sunlight coming across the top of that silvery cloud. Do you see it?"

Anne: "Yes, I see it. It's pretty."

Mary: "It's more than pretty, Anne. It's wonderful. It's a cloud with a silver lining. It's hope. It's promise. It's an opportunity for love and prosperity for us all. Remember this cloud on every rainy day. Remember the light to show a positive way. Remember the rain to make our gardens grow. There's more to life than first meets the eye, if you look for it."

Anne: "Are you telling me that I should be looking at the sky and seeing more than bad weather?" (thinking: This woman has lost it. This is crazy.)

Mary: "In a word, yes. We see what we want to see. If we only think of negative things, and carry a bad attitude, all we'll ever see is storm clouds and trouble. That's all we'll ever think about and that's all we'll get. The weather is what we make of it. (thinking: I've lost her. She must think I'm nuts. How can I ever explain this to her?)

Anne: "Hmm. I think I'm getting this but now let's change the subject before I get a headache. I never knew that the weather could be such a deep subject." (thinking: Is she really saying that we influence the weather?)

Mary: "Anne, have a marvelous weekend. I bet you and Peter will find something fun to do."

Anne: "Thanks. You too. (thinking: I have no idea what Peter and I will do. Weekends are usually a dull drag while we try to avoid chores and having to talk to each other. Anyway, Peter has a game Saturday afternoon. Maybe I can shop even if we can't afford anything.)

Saturday morning at Anne & Peter's house:

Peter, putting the paper down: "I've got to leave early today -- right after lunch. We want to get in a little batting practice before the game. This is a tough team we're up against. What are you going to do today? (thinking: Whatever it is I hope it doesn't cost too much.)

Anne: "I was thinking about going shopping, but I know you're concerned about our budget, so I thought I'd come watch the game. Is that okay or will it interfere with your guy fun?" (thinking: He probably won't want me there. I'll just get in the way when they head off to the bar afterward.)

Peter: "What? You never come to the games. Are you sure you want to come. It might rain." (thinking: She'll probably want to leave early if it starts to even drizzle and that'll ruin the day.)

Anne: "Yes. I'd like to come. I see some sunlight breaking through the clouds so it should be okay. But, I'll bring an umbrella in case it rains. Let's go."

Later at the park:

Peter: "Wow. Did you see that double play? Mark really pulled the game out of the trash at the last second with that catch. I don't know how he even went for it, much less made it. This puts us in third place."

10

Anne: "It wasn't just Mark, although he really put his heart into it. It was the whole team. You guys really seemed to click today."

Peter: "Yeah, it felt good. Everyone had a great attitude today and we really connected as a team. Nobody was complaining about anything for a change. Not even the weather, even though it was cloudy. I feel pretty good. What do you say we go home."

Anne: "Don't you want to go celebrate with the guys?"

Peter: "I'd rather go celebrate with you."

Anne: "Let's go home and talk about the weather."

Peter: "What? Why do that? Let's find something else to talk about."

Anne: "Okay."

At work Monday, on the way to lunch:

Mary: "Well, Anne, I bet you had a great weekend."

Anne: "Yes, Mary, I did. How did you know?"

Mary: "I made a positive affirmation for you. I thought the thoughts and then said the words for you to turn into action. Don't you remember our parting conversation on Friday? You made your own weather."

Anne: "I do remember you wishing me a great weekend but how did you know it would happen?"

Mary: "Anne, I had faith in your ability to turn my positive wish into a positive deed. You did that didn't you?"

Anne: "Yes, I guess I did. I went to one of Peter's games for the first time in a long time. After the game one thing led to another and, well you know, we had a great weekend. We didn't even argue too much until Sunday when I asked Peter about his work. I dropped that subject fast enough so it didn't get too bad."

Mary: "Why did you go to Peter's game after all this time? I thought you hated them."

Anne: "Well, I was thinking about it and I realized that maybe I was jealous -- jealous of his team and the fun they were having while I was home alone. Once I figured that out, it somehow seemed all right for me. I can see how important it is for Peter to have his own activities. To be honest, I was surprised he let me go. I never thought he'd share it with me. Maybe he's not as selfish as I thought."

Mary: "It sounds to me like you made your own weather this weekend. You put water on your flower garden and let some sun through the clouds. Isn't it amazing what you can do in a positive way? (thinking: Maybe there's hope here. Maybe she doesn't think I'm nuts now.)

Anne: "I hate to tell you this, Mary, but last week I thought you were crazy. Now I'm ready to hear more about how to build a positive relationship." (thinking: I'm desperate. One good weekend can't save a marriage. It just reminded me of what we've been missing. Why can't Peter and I talk like this?)

Mary: "We've talked a bit about flowers and gardens and clouds and weather. If you're ready, let's talk about work."

12

Anne: "I'd rather talk about relationships. I've got enough work on my mind between the Jones' project and whatever is going on at Peter's work." (thinking: Let's get to the fix here. I'm desperate. To be honest, I'm not sure how long I'm going to last.)

Mary: "I hate to tell you, Anne, but I'm talking about the art of loving and positive communication in relationships. There's no quick fix. Nothing of real value in life comes for free. You must give to receive. You must sow before you reap. And whatever you sow you will harvest. If you plant weeds, you'll have weeds. If you plant poorly and don't take care of your crops, your harvest will be full of weeds and you may despair. On the other hand if you diligently plant good crops and care for them well, you will harvest the bounty. Plant the seeds of hope, of positive affirmation, and of positive deeds and your wishes can come in many ways. You must have both faith and commitment -- faith that you can do it and commitment to make it happen."

Anne: "Okay I think I understand that I'm going to have to work to follow a positive path but what does that mean? What kind of work do I have to do? What will I get for that work and how will I know it's working for me? (thinking: I don't want to waste my time. Just because Mary's happy now doesn't mean I'll be or whether it'll even last for her.)

Mary: "You've asked a lot of questions. I'll do my best to answer them. I know I was uncertain when I first started working on creating our positive relationship. It took a few months for me to really begin to believe. I guess the first very positive proof I had came when Frank told me he loved me and wanted to work on our relationship with me. I never thought he'd buy this concept. I'd told him about the book but he didn't say much at first. After a while, though, he started noticing little things that I was doing. Little flowers that I was

13

planting were growing. Somehow I was happier, our relationship was a little better and he even said he felt better though he didn't know why. I told him I was working on my positive self and our relationship. I thanked him for noticing and said that if he really wanted our lives to improve, he could help me. That's when I asked him to go to the seminar with me. After that we started talking, talking about loving communications, ourselves and our relationship. It was wonderful.

"Up to that point I planted my flowers and pulled my weeds alone. I did positive things for everyone I could including Frank and never expected anything in return. For a long time I could only go on faith. When nothing came back and my faith was weak, it seemed like only so much wasted hard work. That's not a very positive place to be but my faith carried me through. I hadn't realized it, but Frank was at the same place I was earlier.

"Anyway, that's a long-winded answer to part of your question. Being positive takes faith and work, until it becomes natural for you to do everything in a positive way. Then you must maintain it with care."

Anne: "That's a lot to think about but you know what, I'm going to do just that. I think it's worth the effort. By the way, thanks for the help on the Jones' project. I might be able to get it finished in a couple of weeks."

Mary: "You're very welcome. Please stop by my area at break, I have something for you."

Later at Mary's desk:

Anne: "Hi, Mary, you asked me to stop by."

Mary: "Hi! Thanks for coming by, I wanted to give you this summary of the international aspect of the Jones' project. I had some ideas that I thought you could use."

Anne: "Mary, I don't know what to say. This is hours of work. What do you expect out of it?" (thinking: Are you trying to steal the promotion away from me by making me look bad? Will everyone else know you cooperated on this and somehow I'll look less capable?)

Mary: "Anne, please believe me that this is only a gift from my heart. I was thinking about you and I know how much this promotion would mean to you. I hope you get it."

Anne: "How can you hope I get it when you want and deserve it as well?"

Mary: "I have faith Anne, that what I give I shall receive. If you accept this, you give me the gift of trust in return. That means a great deal to me. I'm working in my garden. Will you work with me?"

Anne: "Yes, I will. I'm a bit confused and overwhelmed by my own thoughts but you've been consistent in what you've said and done for me. I trust you. Thank you. It looks like I have work to do."

A few days later at Anne and Peter's home in the evening after a long hot day:

Peter: "Can't you turn the music down? I've got a lot of work to get done tonight and this noise is annoying. (thinking: I don't know what I'm doing anymore. I just can't seem to think straight with all the pressure.)

15

Anne: "Peter you bought this CD. I thought you liked it."

Peter: "I do, but you play it too loud."

Anne: "I'm sorry, honey, I'll turn it off. Let me get you some cold juice maybe it will help you relax."

Peter: "What do you mean, relax! Do you think I need to relax? Stop bothering me and I'll be okay." (thinking: I don't know what's happening. I feel out of control. I don't know what else to do so here I'm taking it out on you. You've been so nice lately, I feel guilty. I need a drink.)

Anne: "Honey, I'm sorry if I upset you. I'm just trying to be of positive help to you." (thinking: Oh-oh, here you go…trouble.)

Peter: "If you want to help, you can get me a new job when I lose this one." (thinking: She'll never stay with me if I lose this job. She'll see I'm not worth it. Here she might get promoted and I'm only headed down and out.)

Anne: "Peter, I love you. You matter far more to me than any job. I don't care what you do as long as you're happy and we're together." (thinking: I hope he hears me. He's pretty upset.)

Peter: "Anne, I've got to tell you, I think I'm going to lose my job. I don't know what to do. You've been so nice to me lately and I've been a real pain. You've been treating me like we're newlyweds again, while I've been ignoring you. I'm afraid I'm going to lose you."

Anne: "Oh, Peter." Hugging him, "You don't know what good news this is."

Peter: "Are you crazy? This is a disaster and you're telling me this is good news. Have you been drinking?" (thinking: I'm lost and now Anne is, too. We're really in trouble.)

Anne: "Peter, you heard me right. This is good news. You've told me, in so many words, that you love me. You haven't really said that in a very long time. You've also told me, at last, what's really bothering you. I thought you just didn't like me anymore and were treating me badly just to keep me away. We can deal with this. We can work together to save our marriage if that's what you want to do. It'll take work but maybe we can do it. The rest will follow."

Peter: "Anne, I do love you. I've just lost it and it's not the same anymore. What can we do?"

Anne: "The first thing we're going to do is celebrate this moment. It's a silver lining in a dark cloud and we must remember it as we work together on our relationship."

Peter: "I'm not sure what you mean but right now your hugs sure feel good."

Next morning:

Anne: "I really appreciated our talk last night. I hope you feel better. We'll get through this. This weekend I'm going to invite Mary and Frank over. Is that okay? Maybe you can talk about the weather and divert our worries for awhile."

Peter: "Okay but I hope they don't stay long. I've got a lot of work to do. (thinking: We have little in common. I'll be bored and I'll still be behind at work on Monday.)

Later that night at home:

17

Anne: "Peter, honey, I see you're tired and you may not want to talk. Just know that I love you and I'm here for you. I will help you in a positive way and I know that this will all work out well for us."

Peter: "I wish I had your faith. I really don't know what to do."

Anne: "Let's start by looking at where we are. What's the worst that could happen to us? We could get a divorce, you could lose your job or I could lose out on the promotion at work.

"If we commit to each other that we'll work on our relationship and have faith in each other, then the first possibility isn't going to happen unless we choose it.

"You may not be able to control whether or not you keep your job but you can influence it. Even in the worst case, however, if they lay you off, we can certainly get by until you get a new job. If I don't get this promotion, I'll work for the next one. In the mean time, we'll tighten our belts and move to a smaller apartment if we have to. We can be comfortable with a lot less than we have now if we're happy with each other."

Peter: "I hadn't thought of it that way. I just saw us losing everything. Maybe I could even find a better job. Anyway, I think you're going to get the promotion if they give it based on your attitude. I've never seen such a positive attitude."

Anne: "Well, you'll see even more positive attitude Sunday when Mary and Frank are here. Now let's talk about your work."

Sunday afternoon: Frank and Peter are in the yard. Their wives are in the apartment.

18

Frank: "Peter, thanks for inviting us over. We really haven't seen you very much in the past few months."

Peter: "Yeah, work has been hard lately. You know, with the restructuring going on everyone has been worried. I've been burning the midnight oil, although I think I'm the one who'll be getting burned."

Frank: "I know what you mean. Our company went through something like that some time ago. Things worked out for almost everyone, though."

Peter: "How can that be? The ax is the ax and when it hits you you're dead."

Frank: "That can be true but it doesn't have to be. You can take affirmative action and beat the ax."

Peter: "Now, I'm really confused." (thinking: Anne told me Frank and Mary were positive but this makes no sense at all.)

Frank: "Let me explain. It's really quite simple. There were at least three significant positive actions that we could and did take. First a bunch of us took the opportunity to rise to the occasion. When we saw that the company was in trouble, we worked harder and smarter to succeed. Some of us formed problem solving teams and went after the issues at the core. We figured out the worst that could happen, made acceptable plans to handle the worst case, put these plans away since we knew we wouldn't need them, and found better and more acceptable ways to solve the problems. Then some of the managers and workers reassessed their roles in the company and decided it wasn't worth the trouble to stay and fight. They went on to find different jobs where they'd be better satisfied and better contributors.

19

"I talked with Mary about the problems we were facing in our relationship and in life with my job in jeopardy. We worked together on them. We talked a lot. It brought us closer together. We felt so much better once we understood each other and how we could have faith in our mutual commitment to our relationship. It took a long time but here we are.

"Today we do have fewer people in the company but those who remain are happier and more productive. The company's doing well. My marriage is stronger and more fulfilling than it has ever been. Mary and I feel very lucky and very fortunate. We grew a lot through this storm. We now make our own good weather and our flower gardens are flourishing."

Peter: "I was following you until you started talking about weather and flowers. Could you explain what you mean and what this might mean to me and my problems?"

Frank: "Sure, we can talk some more later. I hear the women calling us to dinner."

At dinner:

Anne: "How was your men's conversation? Anything new and exciting?"

Peter: "Anne, you were right about Frank being a positive person. I think we have a lot of learning to do and there are some things I don't understand."

Mary: "Frank certainly is a positive guy today. Don't worry about understanding everything overnight. It took him months of practice."

Frank: "Yeah, that's for sure. But it really helped to have Mary on my team. Speaking of help, Pete, you asked me about how Anne sometimes wants to talk and you really don't feel like it. The more she pushes, the more you want to back away. Like I said maybe Mary and I can give you and Anne a new perspective on that if you'd like."

Anne: "As far as I'm concerned anything will help. When I've got something on my mind, I'm frustrated or just lonely, I want to talk to Peter about it. Sometimes he says he just doesn't want to talk about it then. When I tell him how important it is to me, he just clams up. Sometimes we even end up fighting – over nothing. What's wrong with us?"

Peter: "Now it's not all my fault. There are times when you're just pushing too hard and I feel like you're after me."

Frank: "Don't worry. Nothing's wrong with you. You're just experiencing the pursuit and withdrawal cycle that is a natural behavior that you can learn to work around. I did, well, Mary and I did.

Mary: "We women like to talk about what's on our minds. We like to share our feelings. It makes us feel better. We really like to be close to people and talking and sharing are a way of bonding. We especially like to have an intimate bond with our mates. We can even feel close when we talk about very emotional topics. I think it's a hold over from our ancient heritage when the family really had to stick together for survival."

Frank: Men, on the other hand, have an instinctual desire to defend the family. We go on the alert whenever there is even a hint of danger. Our heart rate actually speeds up when we talk about intimate or emotional issues while the women are cool as cucumbers. They like getting close and we're trying to figure

21

out how to defend ourselves. It's like oil and water for the moment. The more the woman approaches when the man isn't ready, the more he goes on the defensive. Then the woman tries harder, the man retreats more and pretty soon their both frustrated and angry."

Anne: "That makes sense. What can we do about it?"

Frank: "Peter, you can do what I do. When I'm not ready to talk about a problem or an issue, I ask Mary to tell me what she wants to talk about and we make an appointment. That gives me time to get ready and not be defensive. I tell Mary that I love her. That helps anytime."

Mary: "I not only tell Frank what I want to talk about I also limit it to one problem or topic. I keep the appointment short so I'm not asking for too much from him. We don't make appointments for everything. That would be rough. I just make sure that both Frank and I are in the mood to talk when I bring up some touchy subjects like money and the in-laws. Other times I let Frank know that all I really want is for him to listen and understand. I really don't want him to fix anything or even respond. It's just that I want to share with him."

Frank: "Knowing that I don't have to fix everything or take responsibility has made it easier for me to have more conversations. I'm more comfortable now just listening and letting Mary know that I understand. We still have our appointments to work through the tougher issues and we have many more good conversations now – just like we did when we were dating. It's great."

Monday over dinner:

Peter: "I'm still not sure that I understand everything that Frank and Mary have been telling us. I've been nice to everyone at

22

work. I even helped Ralph, you know the real pain in the rear, with his work and all he did was sort of grunt at me. I'm still worried about my job and nothing seems to be working out. I've pushed this positive way about as far as it can go and what do I have to show for it? I'm tired."

Anne: "Peter, one thing we have to remember is that our words and thoughts are things. They're as real as anything, so if you don't want things to work out just say so and that's what you'll get. Let's do a little gardening. I love you and you love me. Right? We can build from there."

Peter: "Yeah, you're right as usual. Frank said that I should be patient while working hard. Please forgive me if I put my burdens on you. It's not fair."

Anne: "Peter, I'm here to share with you. Remember, we're a team now. It does take work to be good team."

Peter: "Yes, sweetheart, and I need more practice. Until we talked about it, I really didn't think about how much commitment and practice it really does take to create a good relationship. Now I know that we can work together with a winning goal in mind. By the way, are you coming to the game this weekend? It's for the championship and I'd really like for you to be there to see us win."

Anne: "I wouldn't miss it for the world. When you've finished with your work after supper, I'd like to talk to you about some problems I have at work. Mary usually helps me but this time she told me to go home and talk to my partner."

Peter: "I'd be glad to talk to you. Two heads are better than one now that we're both thinking and talking."

The next Monday evening at home after work:

Anne: "Don't worry about taking out the trash tonight. I don't want you walking on that ankle any more than you have to. I'm sorry you bruised it sliding home, but it sure did make for an exciting win. When is the awards dinner?"

Peter: "Thanks, honey. It's next Thursday night. I'm sure my ankle will be better by then. Did you talk to Mary about that promotion situation at work? I know you were upset last week when you talked. Is there anything more to the rumor that you got the job?"

Anne: "Nobody's talking but there are sure a lot of whispers. I'll feel bad if I get it after all the help Mary gave me. We talked about it at lunch today and she just smiled and said that we had both done our best and our positive ways will carry us through to the best outcome. She's so positive. I couldn't help but feel good after talking with her. Frank says hello and hopes you can get together next weekend."

Peter: "You know, it's been about a week since we had our last stay at home date and talked about us. I'd like to make a date for Friday night, so we can just talk. I have some questions and I wonder how we might be able to improve our lives some more. We're doing so much better and I think that'll give us more to build on. I have a few weeds left in my garden and I can't seem to get rid of them. I'm working on faith. Faith that we share love and that we can work together. But, it's still hard sometimes."

Anne: "I know what you mean. We did some mean things to each other and sometimes they come back to haunt me. I either feel guilty or angry and I don't like it either way. I don't know how we ever got along with each other. I guess that's why we never talked."

24

Peter: "Well, we were good at fighting. It seems like every time you had something important to say, all those thorns and weeds got in the way. The weather was usually bad, dark and stormy. Speaking of weather, Jack at work, asked me today why I was always so cheerful -- with the rumors and all. I smiled and told him I was changing the weather to make us both happier in spite of everything. I think it surprised him. He was at a loss for words and that's unusual for Jack."

Anne: "That's good. Old Jack seems to always have a sharp comeback for everything and it's usually not very positive."

At home a few days later:

Anne: "Peter, you won't believe what happened. Well, I guess you will when you hear the whole story. I got the promotion to assistant office manager. Mary..."

Peter: "Anne, that's so great. I knew you'd get the job. You were so positive in your approach but what about Mary? We're having lunch with her and Frank Saturday. She must be hurt. She really wanted that job."

Anne: "Peter, don't worry. It's okay. Mary got an even better job. They made a new training job just for her in Human Resources. She's going to spread communication and positive thinking to the entire company. Mary said she's now in charge of weather and gardens and we all have a lot of good work to do together there."

Peter: "Anne, come here. You deserve the biggest hug in the world and then we're going out to Ronzoni's and get some of that ravioli we both love."

Anne: "By the way, it's my treat. I got a dollar an hour raise to go with my new desk."

Peter: "If you don't mind I want to call Mary and congratulate her first. We owe her and Frank a lot and it's so nice to see the good people win."

Anne: "Honey, I agree. I love you so much and respect you for your kindness. Isn't it great to have flowers to give now?"

Saturday lunch:

Peter: "Anne and I are so appreciative of what you've done for us. Anne told me all of the work you did to help her. I'm sorry to say, Mary, that I doubted your motives at first."

Mary: "Peter, that's okay. It seems we're trained to doubt the positive. I don't know why. My joy comes in helping good people like you to live in a more positive way. That's reward enough in itself. Everything else is a bonus that Frank and I accept with grace. We're both so happy for the two of you."

Frank: "By the way, Mary and I made a bundle on that stock I . told you about. Maybe it was luck or maybe that research paid off for us. We're headed out on vacation in August after the dust settles for Mary in her new job."

Peter: "I know you told me to think positively and more would come your way. This happened with Anne's promotion but how do we do what you did?"

Frank: "First you have to think positively and then you have to work your garden. You have to look for opportunities and then study them carefully to separate the flowers from the weeds. It can be difficult and sometimes the small plants you choose turn out to be weeds. But if you're smart about it, you'll earn more than you might lose. Whatever the case, if you don't play the game, you'll never win."

Peter: "Thanks, Frank. I guess I never had the confidence before. Now I'm ready. Better said: We're ready. Anne and I are going to invest at least 10% of our income every month now."

Frank: "How's your work? Is it settling down any?"

Peter: "It's not too bad. In fact, it's good. The boss announced yesterday that business is better and that there won't be any layoff's. There were enough retirements and people leaving for other reasons that we're actually a bit short staffed. I went to my boss and told him that I wanted to take on more work to help out. He said that he was impressed with the offer and that he noticed a real difference over the last couple of months. He said he'd seen my work get better and better. He also said he noticed that others in the group were actually beginning to look up to me. He said that whatever I was doing I should keep it up because it was great. I thanked him but I didn't know what else to say.

"It really wasn't until later when Anne and I were talking about it, that I realized what my boss was seeing. He was seeing my flowers and the weather from my positive approach. The rest of the group was finally responding in their own positive way."

Anne: "We're finally beginning to feel that we're getting what we deserve in life. We have happiness, peace and prosperity where we never saw it before. We give the gift to others and it's returned in its own positive way. Thank you so much for your help."

27

Peter: " You know I've realized that not only do we have to commit to our relationships but we have to really look to the future. When we got married, we never thought about what we were going to do to keep our relationship alive. Anne and I spent more time planning our fancy wedding and honeymoon than talking about building our relationship as life partners. Now, by being more positive and focused in our marriage, we see benefits all around. I thank you two."

Mary: "Remember all we did was offer. It was you who chose to learn and it was you who chose to work. You're the ones who deserve the credit and the blessings. Let's eat."

Chapter Two : How Anne and Peter Saved Their Marriage

Why are so many couples like Anne and Peter in trouble so early in their relationships? And why do most couples finally elect to divorce rather than to stay together? These are key questions that can often be attributed to a lack of positive communications and an inability to deal with the natural conflict of intimacy.

In the story, we felt Peter's and Anne's pain when they weren't communicating with each other. They were both feeling alone and shut out from very important parts of each other's lives. The love that they shared and their other honest feelings were slowly replaced by the feeling that they weren't even married or in love anymore. Not being able to really talk to each other, they each began to doubt their self-worth as well as the value of the relationship. Problems became worse and the pressures added to the disappointment of a fading marriage. Their discussions lacked depth, meaning and understanding and their words were neither honest nor kind. Once the words became unkind, the downward spiral of misunderstanding was all too steep.

Not long after the honeymoon, Anne and Peter gradually stopped talking to each other. And silence, lonely silence, like ivy, poison ivy crept through the garden of their hearts. The newness and thrill of learning about each other was gone. Once passion faded, reality checked in, for life. They now had to deal with the natural everyday feelings that weren't offset by the excitement of passion. It was now more difficult to negotiate who was going to take out the garbage than it'd been to decide where to go on a date. Since they couldn't even talk about the chores, then they couldn't share their feelings about everyday life. The faded passion left a hole in the relationship that they hadn't expected and didn't know how to fill. It wasn't until Anne got a reality check and some very good advice from Mary that she was able to understand what was going on between her and Peter and to make some simple yet important changes in her own behavior. Anne began to realize that there were things that she could do to make a difference. Some of these key actions were:

1. Anne began to regain control of her life by choosing to have a positive attitude and to be more kind and respectful in her thoughts, words and actions.
2. She learned that communication isn't automatic. It's a learned process whether it's positive or negative. That meant then that this was something that she could take action on and she did. She decided to work through her fears and to communicate with more honesty about her feelings.
3. She then took small steps to try to understand what her feelings were and, as appropriate, expressed them carefully so that her husband, Peter, could understand as well. She also was careful to try to understand what Peter was saying and feeling as well. This increased understanding was positive for both of them.
4. She had faith that she could succeed and continued to try even when her early attempts didn't work well.

At the beginning of the story, Anne's and Peter's thoughts weren't consistent with what they were saying. There was a struggle between themselves as individuals, and who they were in the relationship, as well as the depth of their lack of ability to communicate. This unfortunately is common, as couples aren't taught how to communicate with one another. We learn to communicate with our peers in school and at work and we establish some connection before marriage, but little of that prepares us for the realities of life together. Peer to peer and friend to friend communication occurs at a different and usually more shallow level than is needed to negotiate the details of living together in a loving and growing relationship.

The example that was set by our parents is quite often the closest applicable teaching that newlyweds have for learning how to communicate. That's loaded with potential problems. Frankly, many parents don't have good communications skills, so the examples that they set are poor at best and negative at worst, with gardens that are full of weeds. Even with parents who communicate well and lovingly, the children most likely haven't seen the years of work and development that went into its creation. Children miss out on the formative years, when their parents as newlyweds negotiate their understandings and pull the weeds to create their own loving garden of communication.

Anne and Peter had to do something that they'd never consciously done before. They had to pay attention to their communication. They had to realize that they not only had to be careful about what they said but how they said it. They learned to listen and began to demonstrate more understanding in what they said. There was less accusation and finger pointing in their words and more of a self-acceptance of their own feelings and points of view. As a result, they felt better about themselves and each other.

Peter began to notice a difference in the way Anne was behaving and communicating. He became more comfortable and gradually learned how to express his feelings and concerns in a way that both he and Anne could deal with them. Even the difficulties of work were reduced by sharing these concerns. He began to have enough faith in himself and their relationship that he could talk about the things that were really bothering him.

Peter finally found a real teammate in Anne. Together they began to create the boundaries and rules for their own game of love and life. They finally realized that to hurt each other was to hurt themselves. **They found that they were happy to be teammates in life, so they decided to stay together and become closer.**

The love that Anne and Peter rediscovered within themselves and their relationship was actually in a new form. It contained less of the dizzying heat of passion and more depth of understanding. This faith in love created a new confidence for both of them that was seen by many of their coworkers and friends. Their love began to shine again like a beacon; a beacon that gave them both direction in their love and life and offered a supporting glow to others around them. Their friendships were deeper and their positive attitude became an example for all.

This story closes here only a few months after it begins, but in that short period of time, by virtue of hard work and faith with the support of their mentors, Mary and Frank, they have made substantial progress and are on their way to a happier and more loving lifetime relationship.

The ultimate proof of the presence of love in a relationship is the "aliveness" of each person involved.

You can choose whether you want to be "alive" and foster your relationship with faith, commitment and practice in a positive way, or you can choose to stay stuck.

Your world and life are what you make of them with your thoughts, your words and your deeds. You can choose a path or life will choose it for you, then life will happen *to you* instead of you living the life you want. Which do you choose? Do you want to live like Peter and Anne before or after they decided to change their lives in a positive direction?

Here are six ways to help create your own loving garden:

1. Practice the principles of loving, positive communication to create your own loving future.

2. Take off some of the weight and drop the heavy worries and concerns about your past. If you've done a wrong, make it right. Say you're sorry or do a good deed to repair the past. Now choose to live in the present instead of the past.

3. Forgive yourself. You made the best decisions that you could with the information you had at the time. Don't regret them. Learn from them, know that you can do better now and forgive yourself and go on.

4. Enjoy the sunshine -- laugh and relax. Laugh in the rain, and can find ways to enjoy life even when you're wet. Take the good with the bad and grow together with life's lessons.

5. Find the cloud with the silver lining. Look for the good everywhere. Even bad things can provide good lessons. Look at problems as challenges. Instead of saying "That's a problem." Say "That's a challenge."

6. Dance with your future one step at a time. Have a vision and share that vision with your partner. Work on creating a shared vision and set off for the future together.

As you find your own flowers growing, share them. There's a wonderful gift in flowers of kind words and positive deeds. Share them with your loved ones freely. These are gifts to be given and not traded. There can be no expectation of return. Your *giving* is a gift to yourself.

Chapter Three : A New Beginning

Sometimes all you desperately want is for your partner to talk to you. You think or ask, "Talk to me" and yet receive no kindness or understanding. Even in a good relationship there are times when you might feel alone, hurt or misunderstood, and you or your partner may be withdrawn. This doesn't have to mean that your relationship is doomed. Withdrawal is a natural human behavior that can be brought on by many factors, including stress, fatigue or even habit. The understanding and practice of positive communication skills can help you to create the loving communication that you desire. Developing these communication skills provides you the opportunity to come closer together in a new level of understanding.

It's not at all uncommon for even the best marriages or relationships to hit a bump in the road to happiness. It is, in fact, to be expected. Sooner or later individuals in a committed relationship may find themselves asking, "Is this all there is?" Passion has turned down a notch and the relationship is moving into a new phase where each person seeks to establish themselves within this new context. It can be exciting, difficult, intimidating, scary, or frustrating to go through this relationship development. Don't feel bad. This is a natural process and the guidance in this book will help you turn that process in the direction you want it to take for the future of your relationship.

Partners in a positive, loving relationship have learned how to share loving communication with respect, honesty, kindness and understanding. They also share an enduring commitment to one another and to the careful practice of these skills and the art of loving. You now have the opportunity to share in this joy of life.

Positive communication has several characteristics to ensure it is effective and productive for the relationship as well as those who are in it. Often you aren't only trying to communicate a specific message but you are also trying to be sure that your partner cares about you and what's going on in your life and your relationship.

Characteristics that are often used to describe positive, loving communication in a relationship include the following four:

1. The couple always makes time to talk. Each can get their partner's commitment to talk about any subject even if it's just to agree on a specific time to talk in the near future rather than at the moment the topic is first brought up. There's a shared sensitivity for each other so the "right" time can be agreed upon.

2. There's room for disagreement. It's not the absence of disagreement that characterizes the "perfect" relationship but rather how well the inevitable disagreements or conflicts are handled. Acceptance and understanding are as appropriate as agreement and compromise.

3. The couple has reached an understanding on how to communicate to ensure that even difficult matters can be discussed with safety, respect, and kindness. The most difficult topics can be discussed in the safe knowledge that the loving relationship will continue.

4. Each partner feels safe, respected, validated, and strong as an individual. There's a shared understanding of what's truly important to each person, as well as to the relationship.

How individuals handle their differences as a couple may be more important to their relationship than how they

35

accommodate their similarities. Differences lead to conflict and conflict often leads to a breakdown in communication. Once you learn how to communicate in a positive way, you can accommodate your honest feelings of anger, frustration and the like without having to suppress them. You can be yourself while you talk or argue about difficult issues without attacking your partner, your relationship or yourself. **You can have positive communication about negative things. Your relationship can grow stronger as you manage your differences and problems together as a couple.**

You started your loving relationship with the hope and expectation of a lifetime of happiness, comfort, understanding and friendship. What can you do to fulfill this expectation? You can read on and take action on the information provided in this book. There is hope for those who wish to create a new relationship or improve an existing one.

Hope

There's hope when you look to the lessons found in life. Communication that leads to understanding can be the heart of a good relationship. The strength of this loving communication and understanding drives away the emptiness that painful emotions would otherwise rush to fill. Those painful emotions include: loneliness, fear, resentment, anger, hate, rejection and remorse. Without understanding, what began as love can dissolve to loathing or at least separateness.

The greatest fear of all human kind is that of being alone. The second greatest fear is that of losing our self-identity. Our self-identity is who we think and feel that we are. It is the "person" that we know and are comfortable with. We are made up of our personality and behavior. We may feel that our self-identity is being lost if we are asked/expected to act and behave in a way we are not comfortable. Being lost or alone in what should be a loving relationship is especially painful, but don't despair, for there's hope. When you establish positive communication, you can, with mutual work, faith, commitment, and concern for each other create a fruitful relationship.

How do you establish loving and positive communication? You start with yourself. Self-talk is very powerful so you must communicate with yourself in a positive way. Say the following to yourself several times "I'm a loser." How do you feel? Now say the following to yourself several times "I'm a winner." You probably felt better when you told yourself you are a winner. You typically have about 50,000 different thoughts each day. If you work to limit the negative thoughts about yourself and add more positive ones, you will change the way you feel. **You can positively enhance your self-esteem and self love by changing the way you self-talk about yourself.**

Let's listen in on Anne and Mary as they talk about self-talk.

Anne: "I feel so low all the time. My self-esteem is shot. I don't have enough energy to put into my relationship with Peter. I'm ready to give up. I blow up over even the littlest things and the next thing you know we're fighting."

Mary: "I know what you mean. Several years ago, on a scale of 1 to 10, my self esteem was a negative 5. I took all the anger and frustration I felt within out on poor Frank. We were just dragging each other down."

Anne: "You seem to have great self-esteem now. What happened?"

Mary: "Well, the first thing I did was to read everything that I could get my hands on to learn how to develop my own self-esteem. The one common theme that I found was that in order to love someone else you must first accept and love yourself. The other thing that I learned is that *we are who we think we are and we get more of what we concentrate on*."

Anne: "I don't understand. What does this mean?"

Mary: "Whatever we think about becomes reality and I was constantly telling myself that I wasn't good enough. So my own thoughts were like an inner critic that was convincing me that I wasn't any good. I had to stop thinking negatively about myself and replace those thoughts with positive thoughts and affirmations. It took a lot of practice until I found that most of the time I was more positive than negative. As I changed my self talk, my self-esteem improved and so did my life in general."

Anne: "Well, how do I stop my negative thinking?"

Mary: "One word at a time. Awareness is a key. I figured out when I did most of my negative self talk – when I was feeling depressed or down on myself, when I had made a mistake, when Frank and I had argued and when others disapproved of me. I was alert then and listened to what the inner critic was starting to say and then shut her off with a quick 'Stop, I don't need to listen to this.' Then I replaced that thought with a positive one like 'You're OK, Mary. That's just distorted thinking.' Frank and I talked about self-esteem and agreed to stop the criticism and provide support to each other. We learned to choose our words carefully. We've helped each other a lot."

Anne: "Thanks, Mary. I'll give it a try. I do believe that if I feel better about myself, I'll feel better about my marriage. I just didn't know how to start."

Mary: **"Start now. Today is a new day – a new beginning."**

Chapter Four : Where Are You and Where Do You Go From Here?

I mprovement comes through making positive changes in the way that you do things. You can undergo change by understanding yourself and your environment and by developing new skills and behaviors. One golden rule that you must keep in mind while making this journey is: "I can only change myself and not my partner. I can help my partner to understand the options and opportunities but it's up to him/her to change him/herself. Each of us, as individuals, is responsible for our own selves and our own thoughts. No one can make us think or feel anything."

Your heart may tell you that it's time for a change. Change is possible only with your thoughtful and purposeful effort. Improvement through change is a journey that you take. Along the way you'll have the chance to see yourself and your relationship in a new light and to see how you might nourish the garden of your relationship. You can do some serious weeding and fertilizing to grow more flowers in a new and wonderful way.

Where are you?

To start your journey to this new place it helps to understand where you are. You may be in any one of several places in your relationships:

1. **Home Sweet Home**: You have great communication. You are exactly where you want to be with the love and support that you want. You may not even want to go somewhere else. If you already have the joy of a mutually enriching

relationship, we salute you. We hope that you'll read on to gain confidence that you're communicating in a positive and loving way that will allow you both to continue to grow together for a lifetime. This is where everyone yearns to be and we hope that you'll share your knowledge with others as Mary and Frank did so that they may learn to do what you're doing as well. Your relationship is like a garden where your loving words are like lovely flowers that are sweet to everyone. You, as individuals, are happy, satisfied, and strong. You, as a couple, are as one able to withstand the storms of life, to bend, rebound and prosper.

2. **Building**: You don't talk enough. You are in a happy and committed relationship with a desire to improve. This is a marvelous chance for you and your partner to further develop your communication to have a stronger and more fruitful relationship. But, you can see the weeds encroaching and you know that it's time to take action before they take over. Tend your flowers and weed out your bad habits.

3. **Searching**: You don't talk much at all. You question your relationship because it hasn't turned out the way you wanted it to be. The bloom is off the rose and you worry about the future. You may feel caught, unfulfilled and desperate for change. The very fact that you are reading this book shows that there's hope. There may be more weeds than flowers, but we hope you can see at least one flower. Use that flower as your guide and your center of hope even though you may hurt your hands on the thistles that you pull and cast aside. That guiding flower may be found, for example, in the memories of why you committed to one another in the first place. Don't hesitate to share that with your.

4. **Starting Anew**: You're thinking about committing to a new relationship and you want to start in a new positive

direction. You want to be sure that you know which direction to take. Perhaps previous relationships haven't worked out as well as you might have wished and you don't want to take the same path again. It helps to select the right mate but it helps even more to mutually commit to developing a strong bond through positive and loving communication.

Individuals generally have a good sense for where they are but it doesn't hurt to take a look around once in a while. You can do this in your relationships by using the following guides and assessments. Please use them now and then again later whenever called for in this book.

Listening Skills Rating:

How well you and your partner listen is critical to effective communication. This rating is an evaluation of the current level of your listening skills as well as what you perceive your partner's listening skills to be. Please complete the form at this time and, if your partner is working through this book along with you, he/she should do so as well.

INSTRUCTIONS: Think about how often you do the following and write in the number that you think matches that frequency? On a scale from 1 to 5, give yourself a score as follows: 1 = never, 2 = rarely, 3 = sometimes, 4 = often, 5 = very often.

1. I avoid staying on any one subject with my partner.

_____

2. I make assumptions about my partners feelings or thoughts.

_____

3. I respond to my partner's suggestions or opinions with, "Yes, but..."

_____

4. I bring up past issues during current disagreements.

    _____

5. I interrupt my partner's conversation.

    _____

6. I use sarcasm or jokes to respond when my partner talks.

    _____

7. I respond to a complaint with a complaint.

    _____

8. I insult and criticize my partner.

    _____

9. I respond to my partner with phrases like, "That's ridiculous."

    _____

10. I see only my point of view.

    _____

TOTAL (Add up your scores.)

    _____

You rate your *partner's* listening skills: <u>How often do *they* do the following?</u> On a scale from 1 to 5, give them a score as follows: 1 = never, 2 = rarely, 3 = sometimes, 4 = often, 5 = very often.

1. My partner avoids staying on a subject until it is solved.

    _____

2. My partner make assumptions about my feelings or thoughts.

    _____

3. My partner comments with, "Yes, but…" to my suggestions or opinions.

    _____

4. My partner brings up past issues during current disagreements.

    _____

5. My partner interrupts my conversation.

_____

6. My partner use sarcasm or jokes to respond when I talk.

_____

7. My partner responds to my complaints with a complaint.

_____

8. My partner insults and criticizes me.

_____

9. My partner responds to me with phrases like, "That's ridiculous."

_____

10. My partner see only their point of view.

_____

TOTAL (Add up your scores for your partner.)

_____

We suggest that if you or your partner have scored over 22, there's room for improvement in your listening skills. You are probably in the relationship Building mode. If your scores are lower than 22, you may be close to Home Sweet Home and if you are significantly over 22, you are probably Searching.

The next chapters will give you guidance on how to improve your listening skills and your overall communication skills. Recognize that to learn and grow means that you'll need to undergo change in your habits and learn new skills. The farther away from Home that you are, and the more that you are Searching, the more work that you'll need to do to make these changes. We encourage you to continue and to work on your skills with hope and perseverance.

<u>**Fighting Fair Evaluation Guide**</u>:

The following questions are designed to give you some insight into how you and your partner deal with conflict and disagreements together. We recommend that you and your partner complete this form separately and then come together to compare them and have a heart to heart discussion about how to improve the way you, as a couple, handle conflict.

INSTRUCTIONS: Think about how you and your partner handle disagreements and write in the number that you think is representative of how often this occurs. On a scale from 1 to 5, give yourself a score as follows: 1 = never, 2 = rarely, 3 = sometimes, 4 = often, 5 = very often.

1. We fight.

   _____

2. We name call.

   _____

3. Things get out of control when we argue. (One of us gets nasty or abusive.)

   _____

4. There are bad feelings for a long time afterward.

   _____

5. Past issues come up during disagreements.

   _____

6. There's frustration even before we deal with problems.

   _____

7. We forget what we're fighting about but continue to fight.

   _____

8. One of us must win.

   _____

9. We place blame.

   _____

10. Neither of us listens to the other.

   _____

TOTAL (Add up your scores.)

   _____

Some couples find themselves arguing too much or never talking to each other at all about controversial issues. This evaluation guide will give you a sense for whether or not you are handling conflict in a positive manner. If your score is over 21 you have the opportunity to Build and if it's 35 to 50 you are probably Searching. Also, high scores might indicate an environment where there could be abuse. Please be aware of this and seek the appropriate counsel to ensure your well being while you're working on yourself.

Now that you've completed the "Listening Skills Rating" and the "Fighting Fair Evaluation Guide," please continue with the following two short questionnaires.

Satisfaction Index:

Take a moment and thoughtfully answer the following questions. On a scale from 1 to 5, give yourself a score of how much you agree with each statement as follows: 1 = strongly agree, 2 = agree, 3 = neutral, 4 = moderately disagree, and 5 = strongly disagree.

1. I'm happy _____
2. My partner is happy _____
3. I can talk to my partner about anything any time._____
4. We handle difficulties very well. _____
5. I feel like an individual and don't feel repressed._____
6. The future looks bright. _____
7. I'm proud of the way we communicate. _____
8. I look forward to being with my partner. _____
9. My partner understands me. _____
10. I understand my partner. _____

TOTAL _____

If your score is 15 or less you may be Home, 16 to 30 you may be Building, and over 31 you may be Searching. These scoring distinctions aren't absolute, but when you combine this evaluation with the other two scores (listening and fighting) you should be able to have a clearer view about where you are. Now the question is one of motivation.

Withdrawal Questionnaire:

Take a moment and thoughtfully answer the following questions.

1. Do you feel that you and your partner talk enough?
   Yes_____ No_____

2. Can you talk about the difficult subjects as long as it takes to reach a satisfactory conclusion?
   Yes_____ No_____

3. Do you or your partner look forward to talking to each other?
   Yes_____ No_____

These questions are intended to prompt answers to the questions "Are you or your partner withdrawing? Are you avoiding each other when you should be talking?" If you answered "no" you are probably withdrawing and this book will help you understand what might be causing you to withdraw and show you how to reconnect with your partner by using the Couple's Fair Exchange Process and the guidelines for positive, loving communication. The more withdrawing you are, the more likely you are to be Searching.

Take a moment to look at your four scores in relation to where you think your relationship is today. Now, what do you want to do about your current situation? If you can answer this question to your own satisfaction, you've probably found the motivation, the will and the hope to go on. We wish you a good journey.

If you're ready, which means you're feeling a level of safety, comfort and confidence, then it might be a good time for you and your partner to compare the results of these ratings. Use this as an opportunity to review and work on your relationship and your communications by going through the rest of the book together. If, however, you are currently having a great deal of difficulty in talking to one another, you may wish to delay discussion until at least one of you has read the rest of this book and are better prepared to discuss any problems in a more positive way. You'll know when the time is right.

Why are you here -- wherever you are?

The current divorce rate of over 55% and the high rate of failure of other significant non-marital relationships may lead many to feel as though there's little hope and too many failures. In failure, individuals seek to place blame. Here our premise instead is to help you understand where you are in your relationship, and to teach you how to take action for positive change. Understanding is empowering. It allows you to take action based on new knowledge to change your future.

While it's difficult to determine the exact cause of each relationship difficulty, we feel that there's a common thread that runs through many of them. That thread is the fact that rarely, if ever, is anyone taught how to communicate under the pressures of intimate life or even how to love. **Lifelong love doesn't come "happily ever after," but it is created through practice.** Lifelong love is grown through the committed and deliberate actions of two people. Positive, loving communication is a key to this success. We all need to learn how to speak about and deal with the problems as well as the joys of life.

Keeping love alive takes more effort than the natural process of falling into love. Relationship building creates its own set of conflicts as you work through the details of life. Who will pay the bills? The rent is late. Who decides what to buy and when? Is the toilet seat up or is it down? How to tolerate each person's bad manners or annoying habits? Why won't they change? My car broke down. I don't want to visit your mother but I feel compelled. If you loved me you would....

We see hope as well as the need for change and growth in the words of Dr. Erich Fromm, the renowned expert on the psychology of love, who observes: "Love is possible only if two persons communicate with each other from the center of their existence.... Love experienced thus, is a constant challenge; it's not a resting place, but a moving, growing, working together; even whether there's harmony or conflict, joy or sadness...." You, too, can communicate and love as Fromm suggests.

You thought once you got married or committed to each other your love would carry you through. The feelings were so strong you felt invincible. You could handle everything and life was so good. Now you can't even talk to each other about some things without getting emotional or even fighting. You struggle with questions such as these:

How did this happen to me?
Why am I now Building or Searching?
Where did the love go?
What did I do wrong?
What did my partner do wrong?
Aren't we meant for each other?
Why do we fight so much?

The answers are as complex as they are simple:

Simple: Love alone is not enough.

Complex but understandable: Love isn't enough because you must build your relationship based on commitment and good communication. If you haven't yet taken the time and effort to do that building, you're setting yourself up for failure. Courtship brought you together with passionate love. You reveled in the discovery of your similarities and your differences. You probably took little time to build the joint understanding of how you would deal with conflict since that was the last thing on your minds. Your hearts were leading the way. You assumed that love would make all things right. You believed that if a behavior of your partner bothered you, you could change it/him/her. If life got hard, your love would carry you through. The fact is, however, that as the passionate phase of love passes -- and it will for all of you -- you come face to face with life.

Conflict doesn't have to be negative. Unfortunately, however, most people tend to see conflict as a sign that love is fading. That can lead to the belief that either you, your partner or your relationship is inadequate. Feelings of guilt, frustration, and anger can easily flow from this disappointment. Communication becomes more and more difficult as you are caught up in your own disillusionment and can quickly turn into a real mess. It becomes a downward spiral that's hard to escape without taking the actions that you are now -- such as reading *Talk to Me*.

There is no one to blame. The origin of the problem isn't that you are a bad person and probably not that you and your partner are incompatible. The real problem is usually that you just don't know yet how to communicate in an intimate life setting.

49

Intimacy after passion can be difficult unless you've already started to establish good communication based on understanding, kindness, honesty and respect. Such communication and understanding comes only through *deliberate action.*

Other causes: There can be other causes for unhappy relationships such as incompatibility, neglect, lack of commitment, mental illness, drug or alcohol abuse, abusive behavior, intrusive in-laws and more. Improved communication will make it easier to address some of these but if you find yourself feeling out of control without understanding how to recover, you may be advised to seek counsel. Perhaps there can be a clearer view through the eyes of another person. Whatever you do, we suggest that you take positive action for your future well being.

SUMMARY:

You may be Searching in your relationship because you haven't yet been able to create your own loving communication. It's possible to create your own positive, loving communication by using the Couple's Fair Exchange Process and the guidelines demonstrated in this book. It doesn't matter if you are Home Sweet Home, Starting Anew, Building, or Searching, practicing the Couple's Fair Exchange Process and guidelines will improve your communication.

- The Listening Skills Rating Form, Fighting Fair Evaluation Guide, Satisfaction Index and the Withdrawal Questionnaire can help you assess how well you and your partner communicate.

- You now should have a better sense for where you are: Home Sweet Home, Building, Searching or Starting Anew.

You have the opportunity to set your objective for Home Sweet Home.

- The answer to many troubling questions about love is that love alone in not enough.

- **Lifetime love is based on the practice of good communication that enriches both you and your partner.** Understanding this is a key to allow you and your partner to learn how to value your differences and to grow together in spite of the inevitable occasional conflict.

The following chapter guides you through the Couple's Fair Exchange Process.

You and your partner can learn the structured technique that will help you create loving communication.

Chapter Five : The Couple's Fair Exchange Process

It helps to have a shared and positive process for communicating. Even in business meetings there's a need for process rules and guidelines to keep the discussion on track to a successful conclusion. Loving relationship goals are certainly more intimate than those of a work or social group, but that may be the only major difference. A loving relationship is just a small group of two.

How ever you communicate now, it probably follows a familiar process. There are patterns that have been established even if they're unsatisfactory. If they are unsatisfactory, you've probably created your own process without even knowing how you got there. The chance now is to create a new process on purpose. Understanding and using the Couple's Fair Exchange Process will allow you to be more conscious of how you are communicating and to adjust your behavior to be more effective. This process is simple, powerful, and effective. You can use this process to stop endless arguments and start feeling better about succeeding in your communication and your relationship.

The Couple's Fair Exchange Process helps to break through hot or cold emotions, old habits, and other barriers to communication. You can use the process as a guide and an "excuse" for changing behavior whenever you find yourself slipping back. You will no longer have to yell, scream or beg to be heard and understood. You can rely on the process when you don't agree on how to proceed.

Couple's Fair Exchange Process:

This three step process is outlined and described on the next few pages. We will use it throughout the rest of the book in examples so you can learn how to use it yourself.

1. **Equal time: there is an even exchange of dialogue.** This even exchange will break the old argument cycle where you find each other fighting to prove your position is right rather that working together to solve the problem or reach an agreement. You achieve this with the following:

- Listening: All too often individuals can get caught in the trap of not listening to what is being said. Listening for understanding is fundamental to all good communication.. You must stop thinking only about what you are going to say and start making an effort to listen to your partner.

- Taking turns: Rather than focusing on how quickly you can state your position and win the debate, you should make sure that you share the discussion time with your partner. Your focus is on reaching understanding. You have a better chance of success when you take turns. It's fair. When one of you is speaking, you have "the floor." You should present an idea in a few sentences. You and your partner should then use techniques that we will discuss in the next step (2. Seek understanding before making a decision.) to establish understanding before you go on.

- Not interrupting: The urge to interrupt quite often indicates that you aren't listening for understanding. You don't have to agree with what is being said. Your partner has as much right to speak as you do, so wait. If you don't understand what is being said, you should wait for a pause and ask for clarification. It's impolite to push your thoughts on your partner by interrupting. Your partner may ask for "the floor" or you may give it to them when you are ready.

Continue the process of one speaking and one listening for maximum understanding.

- Time-out: Individuals can become too angry, scared, sad or confused to present their ideas clearly. Agree to admit to those feelings and allow them in your partner. Once one partner has stated an inability to continue, the discussion ends for a prearranged amount of time. It can be five or thirty minutes or the time it takes to walk around the block. When the time has passed, the discussion continues.

- Appointments: Some couple's set times each day or week to talk. They may even have a pre-set agenda so there are no surprises. Other couples make appointments with each other to cover important topics. A good request to your partner for an appointment is polite, states the topic and gives choices for the time. For example "Anne, I would like to talk about the budget for our vacation for about fifteen minutes. Would you like to talk now, in about two hours or later after dinner?"

- Agree on a topic to discuss: When there are a lot of open issues or there are several emotional issues, it can be difficult to stay on one subject. You really don't want to be in the habit of getting out of touch and being distracted by other issues. Agree that you will discuss only one subject at a time. Write it down if you have to and refer to it if the discussion goes off course.

- Agree to try to reach a conclusion: Having an agreed goal in mind -- a conclusion -- will help keep you focused. Without a goal, discussions may tend to drag on or just burn out. You don't have to agree with each other. Sometimes the best conclusion is that you will respect each other's position and agree to disagree.

- Stay on track or get back on track with the Process: Old habits or strong emotions may interfere with using the Process. When this happens, restate the Process, reach agreement to follow it and go on. Using "the floor" to manage the process works well especially when you are under stress. Some people even exchange a piece of floor tile or a piece of paper with "the floor" written on it as a visible symbol of who is supposed to be talking and who is supposed to be listening.

- Set boundaries and rules: Neither of you have to live with abuse or other unsatisfactory behavior. Set boundaries that you are comfortable with. If things get out of hand, you can say "Stop. That is something I (or we) can't accept." *Talk to Me* presents guidelines that you can draw from to create your own rules, the ones that work best for you. An example might be that you both agree to not talk about "hot" topics without an appointment or you'll not bring up your problems until you both have had a half hour to relax after getting home from work. One rule should be that you agree to follow the Process and the guidelines.

2. **Seek understanding before making a decision**: Walk in your partner's shoes before you go too far. Use any or all of the following three techniques to gain understanding.

- Paraphrase: Paraphrasing is to repeat back what you have just heard in your own words. You can say "If I understood correctly, what I heard you say is ...." and repeat what you heard in your own words and then ask, "Is this correct?" You don't make a judgment good or bad, you merely verify to your partner that you heard them correctly. This reduces misunderstanding and shows your partner that you care enough to try and understand his/her point of view. This validation or confirmation is a wonderful gift to give your partner at no cost to yourself.

55

- Clarify: If you don't understand all of what has been said, paraphrase what you think you heard and ask your partner to clarify. You can say, for example, "I think I heard you say ... but I am unclear about your thoughts on .... Could you please help me understand?"

- Give effective feedback: Feedback gives your partner a chance to explain if there are any misunderstandings. Feedback consists of telling your partner what your reaction is to what has been said. You should tell him/her that this feedback is based on what your understanding is and use the following three rules to giving good feedback. It must be:
  - immediate
  - honest
  - supportive, and not attacking (non judgmental).

3. **Throughout the discussion, follow these guidelines**: If you think and speak with these four guidelines in mind, you can't go wrong. Each guideline is discussed in detail in separate chapters.

- Understanding: Understanding yourself, your partner, and what is positive for the relationship.

- Kindness: Communicate in a caring way, even when the topics are serious. Be sure the intent of your message is well meaning and doesn't contain a negative hidden agenda. A hidden agenda is another intent that may not be obvious.

- Honesty: Honesty starts within as you examine your feelings and thoughts, to ensure that you are being truthful to yourself and the relationship. Part of honesty includes saying the right thing at the right time. Timeliness of communication is critical in that *sometimes not saying something is as bad as not telling the truth.*

- Respect: If everything is thought, said and written with respect for yourself and others, there can be little chance for negative communication.

The Couple's Fair Exchange Process is both a guide and a safety net. Read the following example of the Couple's Fair Exchange Process being used by our fictional couple, Anne and Peter, as they work toward fixing some problems in their communication. Anne has read this book and mentioned it to Peter, but he's reluctant to change the status quo, even though it isn't a very happy one.

Anne: "Peter, I know you might not be comfortable with talking about this but I'd like to spend just twenty-five minutes with you later to talk about how we might be able to improve our communication. Would you be willing to do that at eight p.m. or is nine better for you?"

Peter: "I'm too tired for another argument over this. Can't we put it off?"

Anne: "I understand you don't want to fight over this and I agree with you. If I promise to end the discussion if it gets too hot for either of us, would you be willing to give me the time tonight."

Peter: "Well, if you agree to that, I guess so and eight is better than nine for me. Now I'm going to watch the news. Okay?"

Eight p.m.:

Anne: "Peter, I know you're tired and have a lot on your mind. Thanks for sitting with me. I agreed I wouldn't argue tonight. Would you be willing to agree to the same terms that if the discussion gets too hot for either of us, you can end the discussion?"

Peter: "Okay. I really don't need another hassle to worry about."

Anne: "Good. I know my usual approach to telling you what's on my mind seems to put a lot of pressure on you. I'll also make another commitment to you so you won't have to worry about a fight. I'm willing to do most of the talking and I don't even expect you to agree with me. All I ask is that you tell me when you don't understand what I'm saying. I'll do my best to help you understand what I'm saying without any pressure on you to agree. Is that okay?"

Peter: "You mean you don't want me to agree with you; you just want me to listen and tell you when I don't understand? Is that right? Sounds weird to me, but I'll give it a try."

Note: This is an example of paraphrasing. Peter is doing what Anne asked and has demonstrated.

Anne: "Yes, thanks. I've been doing some reading on the subject of couple's communication and I'm beginning to understand some things that might make it easier for us to talk, even about the difficult things. I realize we've been through a lot together in the last year with problems here at home and at work. I didn't realize that being married would be so much work and I guess that I wasn't prepared well enough."

Peter: "Hey, are you saying we shouldn't have gotten married? That's a rotten thing to say."

Anne: "No. That's not what I'm saying at all. Please let me clarify what I've said. I love you and I'm glad we're married. Thank you for holding up your part of the agreement to ask for clarification. I know I've said some cruel things in our past fights that I never should've said, and they might lead you to read things into what I'm saying now. But tonight I'm working hard just to explain things."

Peter: "All right, but what did you mean when you said you weren't ready to get married?"

Anne: "What I meant is that I wasn't prepared well enough to know how to be a good partner in a married relationship. I knew how to be a good date and a good lover and so did you. That seemed to come naturally. What I didn't know was how to work with you, my partner, to establish a good set of rules and guidelines for our communication. I didn't know that it would take effort to learn how to talk to each other about all of the things that go on in our married life."

Peter: "I don't understand. We talked a lot before we got married and we still talk a lot."

Anne: "We did, but we just don't seem to be talking well enough these days. We argue more than we make up. Don't you agree?"

Peter: "Yeah, but it's not my fault."

Anne: "Yes, that's true. It isn't your fault and it isn't mine. We just have to learn how to communicate differently."

Peter: "Well, any change might be better, but I don't want to think about it now. Can we quit?"

Anne: "Yes. I promised. Thanks for talking with me. Can we do this again?"

Peter: "Yeah, if we can stick to these rules."

Anne and Peter have said a lot to each other in this short Fair Exchange conversation. They've set some rules, tested them, and are now poised to have another conversation. Is their relationship fixed? No, there's much more to be done to establish their new communication. But notice that even in this simple exchange they were already working on the relationship by working toward trust and understanding. They both acknowledged their past feelings and problems while taking steps toward each other. These are positive steps that can add up and continue if they choose.

How you can use the Couple's Fair Exchange Process to create your loving communication:

1. Determine where you are now. What was your satisfaction index from the questionnaire in Chapter 4? The lower your score, the higher the likelihood that you've already worked out some of the key Couple's Fair Exchange Process rules with your partner. Use this self assessment as a beginning point for your own understanding.

2. Ask yourself what rules you follow in your relationship now that are obviously supportive of both you and the relationship. Example rules include not interrupting, no surprises and time for both to talk. Make a list of them in light of the following questions:
   - Have you both agreed to them or are they just understood?
   - How well do you follow them?
   - Are there some rules that you feel need to be changed to more closely fit the Couple's Fair Exchange Process? Use this list later when you are ready to discuss rule setting with your partner.

3. Establish the use of the Couple's Fair Exchange Process with your partner. Determine what some of the basic rules you feel are most important to you at this time and work toward establishing them with your partner in your relationship. Some rules or boundaries can be set on your own. You may, for example, set boundaries on what types of communication behavior you will or will not accept. Shouting, bullying, and name calling are examples of behaviors that may cross your boundaries. This is especially important in reducing or avoiding abuse.

4. If you aren't talking enough, ask your partner for appointments to talk about things that are important to you. Tell him/her what is on the agenda and why it is important to you. Suggest alternative times. Don't ambush your partner by bringing up a "hot" topic without any warning as that may cause a block to communication.

5. Discuss how decisions will be made. Describe and seek agreement on the types of decisions that you want to be involved in with your partner (for example: paying bills, food shopping, dish washing, house cleaning or social planning). Use agreement and understanding rather than intimidation, insinuation or similar manipulation to make key decisions.

6. Establish a ground-rule that either partner can call a "time-out." This can be done at any time in order to cool off. Then you can get back to the topic at a future agreed specified time when emotions are cooler.

You may wish to refer back here once you've practiced the skills and guidelines in the later chapters to build more confidence in your newly created communications skills. The following discussions on style and power will help you further with understanding and using the Couple's Fair Exchange Process.

Fair Exchange Style - Hot or Cold or Ideal?

Emotions are important to any relationship. Some relationships are hot with a lot of deep feelings and emotional exchanges, some are colder with cooler feelings and emotions, while some are both. You must have emotions to be alive and to love. How do you deal with the extremes in a relationship?

Hot: Do the "rules" of the Couple's Fair Exchange Process mean that, if your communication is intense to the point that it's stormy, you have a bad relationship? No, it doesn't necessarily mean that. Some good relationships are more intense than others. For some couples, voices are raised and emotions are high in love as well as in debate. Those couples make up as passionately as they argue. **The most important key to a stable relationship is that positive words, acts and emotions are shared at least five times more often than any negativity that's shared.** If you have this type of relationship, you may be more comfortable with adapting these rules and behaviors to your own to reach a more positive and satisfactory balance. Do seek a balance. Hot relationships experience extremes like thunderstorms or drought. You hope that the average keeps you growing and the wild changes don't kill the flowers.

Even heated discussions can be made to allow for an even exchange, validation and understanding.

Peter: "You know, Anne, I just don't understand our neighbors Dave and Sally. The way they were yelling at each other last night, I thought they were going to wake up the neighborhood. And today you're telling me that their planning a second honeymoon. What's going on with them?" —

Anne: "Sally tells me that their fights are hot and heavy but they make up just as passionately. They thrive on the energy. She told me that they don't fight very often but when they do it's wild. I guess it works for them."

Peter: "That still doesn't make sense to me."

Anne: "Sally says their positives outnumber the negatives. They really do work to keep their love alive. When they need to discuss some difficult topics they use a technique like 'the floor' to keep the discussion on track. They make sure that they understand each other and they never use abusive language."

Cold: Some individuals or relationships are more distant and cool. They may be characterized by a lack of conflict and avoidance. While there's little obvious negativity, there's a coolness in the love as well. The individuals may be cohabiting and coexisting rather than sharing, loving, and growing. A cold relationship is like a garden that rarely sees the warm sun. It grows slowly, if at all, and may be on the verge of dying if there's a frost. When something difficult comes up in life, as it usually does, these couples may not know how to communicate with each other to handle it.

If you have this type of relationship, you may wish to adapt the rules and behaviors to aid you in dealing with conflict. You should also practice talking so you will know how to talk when you really need to.

Peter: "My Mom and Dad have never talked much in the thirty years they've been married. They seem to avoid most of the difficult issues and I don't know how they ever make a decision. One time, when Dad was laid off from his job, Mom finally got him to talk about it by writing him a note telling him she loved him and that she knew they would work things out together."

Anne: "What happened then?"

Peter: "Dad thought about it for a few days. He told Mom he loved her too. They talked about some places to look for a job and Dad went out and got hired. They avoided conflict when they could but always found a solution together even if it was done quietly over a period of time. Mom did say that she wished they would talk more. She had to start most of the more serious conversations. Dad would sometimes say he didn't want to talk about it, whatever it was. But a day or so later he'd be ready to talk. They do love each other but they're not openly affectionate."

Anne: "Thank you for sharing that with me. It helps me understand what your communication role models were. I can see why you'd rather avoid conflict sometimes. Your parents gave you that example."

Peter: "You're right and I want us to have a better relationship than I grew up with. It's difficult for me to break the habit sometimes. I appreciate your understanding."

Ideal: The ideal is what you create so that your life and relationship are predominantly positive. The emotional climate of your relationship may be hot, cold or in between. Feelings are shared but you still feel secure and you both can still grow because the positive communications that you share with your partner outnumber the negative by five to one. This "magic" ratio has been recently established by Dr. John Gottman, a renowned marriage researcher who has invested over twenty years into the question of what makes a marriage stable. Research confirms that the ratio is more important than the style of the relationship. The Couple's Fair Exchange Process can help you achieve the "magic" ratio.

Power:

Power plays a major role in a couple's communication. Who says what when, and who makes the decisions are key elements in establishing communication behaviors. Any change in communication may be seen as an attempt to change the power structure of the relationship -- and that may very well be appropriate. When you say, "You never listen to me," are you also saying, "My opinion doesn't count" or "I can't make any decisions around here?" The Couple's Fair Exchange Process creates a forum where both sides are heard and acknowledged. This will have a real impact on how important decisions are made.

Two of the challenges of any couple are leadership and decision making. It's easier to reach an agreement on these early in the relationship. If you are in a long standing relationship with a lot of bad habits such as bad or no communication, however, take things one step at a time and go forward on your journey. One of the key advantages of the Couple's Fair Exchange Process is that you can use it to establish a dialogue that's moving toward understanding where none has existed. You will then be able to create a balance of power that you are both comfortable with.

Rules and structure:

All of your communications in any group or relationship can be enhanced by the appropriate use of rules. Business carries its own set of expectations and rules which make it easier for groups to achieve success. In fact, in many of the better companies, team members and managers are taught how to work through team development in order to be productive. Many couples, unfortunately, never make it through the stages of team development with their partner. One reason for this is the lack of awareness on the part of the couple that *conscious action* is generally required to create the rules for working together in a way that is effective and comfortable for both of them. The guidelines for positive, loving communication that follow in the next chapters will help you create your own structure in a positive way.

SUMMARY:

You can create your own version of the Couple's Fair Exchange Process. In doing so, you can feel better about yourself as an individual, your partner and your relationship. These positive actions and feelings are vital to the life of the flowers within the garden of your relationship. You only need five flowers for every weed and the garden can still prosper.

The Couple's Fair Exchange Process works like tending the garden. You reap what you sow. The following chapters in this book provide the guidelines for communicating that will add power and success to your use of the Couple's Fair Exchange Process which include:

- Use the Couples Fair Exchange Process
- Equal time
- Seek understanding before making a decision
- Follow the guidelines
- Understanding
- Kindness
- Honesty
- Respect

Following are six ways that you can use the process:

- Determine where you are now and where you want to be
- Create your own rules and guidelines
- Start using the Couple's Fair Exchange Process
- Set appointments to talk
- Discuss how decisions will be made
- Use time-outs to keep things cool enough

Use the Couples Fair Exchange Process to help you keep your love alive.

Chapter Six : Communicating in a Positive Way -
Guidelines for Loving Communication

Sometimes individuals go on for years in a relationship and wake up one morning to realize that they are alone. Somehow they've lost the bond they once shared. They look for it, mourn it, and lament that love is lost. They ask their partners where the love went, to find that both only know it's gone. It just left in the night when no one was looking and all that is left in its place is the empty loneliness that brings sadness, disappointment and anger.

You have to work hard to prevent this in the first place and even harder to fight your way back to a new place where you can understand each other and share life in a positive and loving way. While there's a lot to life and a lot to communication, practicing these principles of positive communication can bridge the gap to new understanding and a stronger loving relationship.

- The questionnaires in Chapter 3 should have given you a better view for where you are in your relationship -- Home, Starting Anew, Building or Searching -- as well as a better understanding of how you arrived at that place. Here and now you can choose to find your love again through the creation of loving and positive communication. While there's no doubt that it can take a lot of practice, you can also be sure that you are likely to be more effective in sharing your love and your life with others if you communicate by using the Couple's Fair Exchange Process along with these <u>Four Guidelines for Loving Communication</u>:

1. Understanding: Understanding yourself, your partner and what is positive for the relationship.

2. Kindness: Communicate in a caring way even when the topics are serious. Be sure the intent of the message is well-meaning and doesn't contain a negative hidden agenda.

3. Honesty: Honesty starts within as you examine your feelings and thoughts, to ensure that you are being truthful to yourself and the relationship. Part of honesty includes saying the right thing at the right time. Timeliness of communication is critical in that sometimes not saying something is as bad as not telling the truth.

4. Respect: If everything is thought, said, and written with respect for yourself and others, there can be little chance for negative communication.

You cannot pick and choose from the above list and keep only those you find convenient at any point in time. You must use all of them. If you make a mistake and try to avoid a repair, it will sooner or later catch up with you and possibly become a problem in and of itself. Remember that your partner is aware of what you are doing, as well as saying. Also remember that your own conscience is at work at all times. If you make a mistake, simply correct it quickly.

Take a moment and imagine a conversation with anyone during which you are both applying these simple principles: Understanding, Kindness, Honesty, and Respect. Isn't it hard to think of anything less than a positive conversation? Even if you are talking about difficult things it's hard to argue if your foundations are based on kindness and respect. When you add commitment to understanding and honesty, you can accomplish anything. And, since you're talking when it's timely, you are both prepared and the problem has not grown out of proportion by neglect.

Here is an example of a problem stated without and then with these principles in mind:

Without: "You selfish jerk! You never help out with the kids. You promised me a break so I could have a night out. Now I have to take the kids to soccer. How do you expect me to do it all?"

Response: "You're always criticizing me. I'm breaking my back here and all you want is time off. I don't care what you do."

With: "I'm disappointed that you have to work late again but I appreciate how hard you work. I was planning on bowling with the team tonight. Do you have any suggestions on how we can work this out so it's a win-win for us?"

Response: "I'll call our neighbor to see if they can take our kids to soccer practice with theirs. I'll agree to pick them up after practice and bring them home. I can watch for a while and then take them all out for ice-cream on the way home."

These important principles of communication are based on natural human desires, including the need to be understood. Unfortunately, rarely is anyone taught these principles and no one has the chance to see them demonstrated. These common sense principles aren't so common. It's up to you to understand, learn and practice them. As logical as this all is, it still takes practice every day to master the art of positive communication.

One of the realities about practicing these principles and the associated skills is that some mistakes are to be expected. Yet since both you and your partner are working toward the same goals in the same way, you'll both forgive each other's minor omissions. You'll also be able to talk about the principles and how well you are doing in following them. If you do this in a non-critical way, you can discuss just about anything. Even if you're reading this book first without your partner, remember to follow the guidelines and your mistakes will be small ones that you can easily correct. One caution: remember that it's you and your relationship that are most important, not some set of rules. Use what works for you in the way that's best for you.

Here are Peter and Anne stumbling and then catching themselves.

Peter: "Anne, you forgot to enter some checks in the book and now the car payment check bounced!"

Anne: "What do you mean? It's your responsibility just as much as it is mine. Don't get on my back about it!"

Peter: "You're right, sweetheart. I'm sorry I snapped at you. Please forgive me. Do you have a few minutes to help me sort this out?"

Anne: "I forgive you. I'm sorry too. I'll be happy to help you figure this out when this TV show is over. Is that okay?"

It also helps to practice some positive, loving words and phrases such as the following that recognize your responsibility for your personal feelings while they seek to understand and acknowledge those of your partner.

I love you.
I'm sorry for (name it).
Please.
Thank you.

Please help me understand how you feel.
I care.
I'm willing to (name it).
I'm committed to (say it).
I understand.
Remember the good times.
How may I help you?
I'm feeling (state how you feel).
Let's work on the problem together in a positive way.
I respect your opinion. My opinion is (state it).

If you are having a difficult time saying positive words such as these, try writing short notes to your partner. Try them out and see what happens. It may take time, but as you change for the better, you'll have a positive influence on your relationship. Have faith that you can achieve your goals. Good intent starts the journey and practice makes perfect.

SUMMARY:

- Understanding, Kindness, Honest and Respect allow positive communication.

- If you make a mistake, correct it quickly.

- Remember to forgive each other minor omissions.

- Use positive, loving words and phrases or notes to maintain a positive influence on your relationship.

When you validate your partner's feelings and share understanding, kindness, honesty and respect, you two can talk about anything.

Chapter Seven : Understanding

Understanding is a universal human need. You may even tend to measure your self-worth to a great extent by how much you think others value you in that understanding. Understanding of another person comes from good listening. If you first seek to understand the other person and then to be understood yourself, you'll have a much better chance of success in your communication. You'll achieve your fullness as an individual and as a couple only with understanding. Further, if you don't listen to yourself, you'll never understand and know yourself.

You know your partner only to the degree that you understand them and they will know you only to the degree that he/she understands you. Understanding comes primarily through how you act with each other and through talking -- what you say and how you say it.

Passion may exist without understanding but enduring love cannot. That's one reason people sometimes find themselves in trouble after the heat of new romance wears off. You have to learn who you are again and find yourself and your partner in this new relationship in a new way. Meanwhile you have expectations and history that get in the way. You expect that loving, understanding communication should flow as naturally as it did during courtship. You expect this to go on forever and are disappointed in yourself and your partner when it does not.

Sometimes even your own emotions and feelings are hard to understand much less your partner's. You may sense what these feelings are, and that they are in the way, but without clarification, you may be wrong. You owe it to yourself, your partner, and the relationship to seek to understand the truth before you leap to judgment with bad assumptions.

You must seek to understand and not to place blame. Understanding is empowering. It allows you to take action today based on new knowledge to change the future. Blame is defeating as it lives only in the past. If you're not in a blaming mode, don't go there. If your communication already contains blame, it's important to intentionally remove blame and to work toward understanding by following the guidelines for positive, loving communication.

You can do better. You can get out of the traps that you may have fallen into. Soon enough you can avoid these traps. With enough practice you can build the depth of understanding that you crave.

Filtering what you hear

So often, though, you speak and aren't heard; you listen but don't hear. Filtering changes what's said into what you *think* you hear. You are so practiced in filtering what you hear -- and think -- through your own thoughts and history that you never truly hear much of what is said. What you think you understand quite often bears no resemblance to what was said or what was intended. How many times have you been in a conversation where you were saying one thing but the other person seemed to be hearing something else? It happens all too easily.

If you expect to hear a negative initial response from your partner and they say something positive you may never truly understand what they have said. You've probably experienced those times when the conversation or argument has gone around and around generating nothing but ill will and frustration, only to end up with an agreement that could have been there all along. Neither party took the time during the conversation to clearly understand what the other person was saying. You hear what you expect to hear and that may not be what is intended.

Especially when there is conflict, you'll tend to fall back on history, habits, and your own state of mind to make an interpretation. If you're feeling negative, your interpretation will be negative. This is another reason why it's important to build and maintain positive listening and understanding skills. The following are some tips and techniques to use to enhance your listening skills.

Listening skills: When you're in a conversation or you're just trying to put your own thoughts together so that they will be clear, you can use some of the following techniques:

- <u>Paraphrasing</u> is a good way to show your partner that you've really listened to him/her. It quite often leads to a better understanding while he/she will see that you value what he/she is saying. When there's a natural pause in the conversation, you restate briefly what you heard by rephrasing in your own words. You also have a chance to get through your filter to a better understanding. Here is an example of a couple using paraphrasing:

  Peter: "There's no way that I can do this any more. You don't care what I have to say. I've had it up to here."

  Anne: "Am I correct in understanding that you're frustrated and that you don't think that I listen to you?"

  Peter: "Yes. I'm frustrated because you don't seem to understand me."

Anne: "Do you think if I were to take more time to understand your point of view and to show you that I care that this would reduce your frustration?"

Peter: "Yes, that'd go a long way. I think you do care for me; it's just that sometimes it's hard to see that, without a little extra effort."

Anne: "I'm glad to hear that you understand that I care for you. I can see that it'd be better for me to make the effort to be sure that I understand you, and that you understand that I care for you."

The simple act of repeating back what you understand in your own words demonstrates that you care enough to be listening. This is validation for your partner that the conversation has importance for you. It's a simple gift to give in good times and a great gift to give if you've been in conflict. It also gives you a chance to be sure that you truly do understand what is being said.

- Clarification is also a good technique for practicing active listening. Ask for clarification on anything your partner said that you don't quite understand. Ask questions. Asking your partner to explain his/her feelings helps draw your partner out to be more open. Keep the conversation going until it's clear you've understood your partner. For example:

Peter: "Don't get mad. I know it's really important to you but I don't think that we should go to your parent's house for Thanksgiving this year. In fact, I don't think that we should go anywhere. I'm tired of all of the traveling and running around and not being able to have a real Thanksgiving of our own. It's such a hassle."

Anne: "Please let me see if I understand. Are you suggesting that we shouldn't have Thanksgiving this year with my parents?"

Peter: "No, I'm not saying that. I just think that we should do something on our own this year."

Anne: "Are you thinking that it would be better to have everyone over to our house this year instead of traveling?"

Peter: "Yes, that's it. If you'll help me, we can have a great time and build a family tradition for the children."

Anne: "I understand. I thought you didn't want to celebrate here because of all the work. I can see now that we can have a great Thanksgiving here if we all work together as a family."

Note that in this example there was no argument. Anne made sure that she understood Peter before she reacted. When she did respond it was to make a suggestion that helped them both reach a good decision on what to do differently about Thanksgiving.

When history is getting in the way of understanding, stop for a moment, clear your mind, and ask the person kindly to repeat what they said because you missed part of it. You may repeat what was said as you think you heard it and ask him/her if that was correct. If it wasn't, seek clarification.

- Effective feedback gives your partner a chance to explain if there are any misunderstandings. Feedback consists of telling your partner what your reaction is to what has been said. You should tell him/her that this feedback is based on what your understanding is.   Remember to use the following three rules to giving good feedback.

1. It must be immediate.
2. It must be honest.
3. It must be supportive and not attacking or mean.

Here are some examples of effective feedback:

Anne: "I really hate it when you ignore me like that. Don't you love me?"

Peter: "Of course I love you. I'm concerned when you use such harsh words. They seem so unkind. Are you saying that you're upset with me or is it that you're uncomfortable with the fact that I'm working on this project right now? My work is important to both of us."

Anne: "Well, yes. I think you work too much at home and that you're ignoring me."

Peter: "I understand. I'm not happy that I have to bring work home. But, we do have bills to pay and I'd appreciate it if you could discuss this without using hard words and bringing our love into question. Would you like to talk about that?"

Anne: "Oh, I'm sorry. I really do appreciate your hard work but I'm lonely when you're caught up in your work. I'll let you finish what you're working on and then we can relax together for a while. How's that?"

Peter: "Thanks for sharing your concerns with me. I'll look forward to the break."

Anne: "Thanks for listening to me. I feel better now."

Note how Peter was careful to tell Anne how he was feeling about her harsh words. There was no angry reaction, just a statement of how he felt and a request for better understanding -- which they reached.

Here's another example:

>Anne: "Look, I've had it with your lazy friends. All they ever do is come over here, stay up late, drink our beer and make a mess. What are you going to do about it?"
>
>Peter: "That's a mean thing to say about good friends. I thought they had a good time last night."
>
>Anne: "They deserve it."
>
>Peter: "Are you still tired or do you truly think that I should call them, wake them up, and get them over here to help clean up? Can we be more positive about this?"
>
>Anne: "Well, I just don't want to clean up this mess myself with this headache."
>
>Peter: "For a moment there I thought it was you and not your headache talking. That must be a mean headache. Would you like to take some aspirin and lie down while I clean this up?"
>
>Anne: "Yes, please. That'd be great. I'm sorry I was so nasty. Thanks for your help. I do love you even if I'm a bit hung over."
>
>Peter: "I love you too and I hope you'll remember this when I ask you to slow down on the drinks next time."

Anne: "I will."

Peter helped to avoid a fight by helping Anne realize that her headache was really effecting how she felt and what she said. The feedback was clear and helpful.

Another example—when history gets in the way.

Peter: "You never listen to me."

Anne: "I told you that I was trying to listen to you and I think I've been doing pretty good. Why are you mad at me now?"

Peter: "Well, every time I talk about getting a new car you get upset."

Anne: "What did I say this time?"

Peter: "I don't remember but it just seems like you never listen to me."

Anne: "I thought I was listening to you. Maybe you assumed that I wasn't because I really just didn't say much. Is that possible?"

Peter: "I guess you're right. I'm sorry."

History is a foundation, but it can also be a trap when you're trying to create a new future. Understanding where you're both coming from can allow you to make choices for the future. But each partner should be careful about what he/she chooses to remember and how those choices influence each person's thinking. Old habits and patterns may be hard to break while you are working to create new ones but you can succeed.

- Be Aware of Body Language:

The meanings of the words you use depend on how you're saying them and the context that they are in. Up to 90% of your communications can be visual. You're receiving not only words but, most importantly for relationships, you're receiving body language and tone. Just try saying "I love you" with a hard face and hands on your hips. Trying to convince your partner that your body language relates only to the physical pain in your back and not your state of mind, you'll see that most often body language prevails over words.

Learn to listen with empathy, openness and awareness. Be aware of the body language and tone of voice that both you and your partner are using. If you sense a discrepancy between what is being said and what you see, ask for clarification. Practice and you'll soon become accustomed to having a free exchange of conversation with your partner with the confidence that if either of you doesn't understand something, you'll seek clarification. Absorb this confidence and take it on for yourself and your partner. It feels good.

With a commitment to achieving and maintaining common understanding, all communications are easier and more loving. Try it. You'll both like it. Remember that you don't have to agree you only have to understand. With that understanding and kindness, you'll make the right decisions.

SUMMARY:

- Understanding is a central part of creating positive, loving communication. With understanding, you can create not only conversation but also true love.

- Some skills to use to ensure understanding and reduce filtering are:

- Paraphrasing
- Clarification
- Effective feedback
- Make sure your body language and words match.

Self-understanding is a power.
Understanding others is a gift.
Understanding your partner is a gift of love.

Chapter Eight : Kindness

Kindness begins in the heart, carries through the soul, and shines in everything that you do. You can do anything together if you do it with shared kindness. Kindness along with courtesy and apology will bring power to your relationships. The most difficult of things in life can be made easier when you share the task with a partner. In kindness, harsh words are never spoken with hurtful intent. With kindness your dreams can become reality and your life rich with love.

Kindness is the expression of caring. You cannot love without caring. And when you share kindness you cannot help but share love.

How can you expect to communicate in love if you don't communicate with kindness? You cannot. So you need to decide to change that.

How can you expect to talk or argue about the bills, a mother-in-law or share a difficult feeling if you have to be kind? Isn't this impossible? It may seem impossible but, in truth, it's only very difficult and not impossible when you follow these simple rules.

- You must remember that you love each other. Work to maintain the safety of that love.

- Remember that the problem is not your love. Direct your anger or frustration to the problem and not your partner.

Yes, you may be arguing about your partner's behavior but even that's not the person. It's just a behavior. If you attack the person, however, you're attacking the relationship and yourself. You must remember that you have to maintain your self-respect as well as that of your partner.

Yes, you may have strong feelings that you must express. But if you express your honest feelings with respect and kindness, you can achieve understanding without planting weeds in your relationship garden. Here is an example of kindness in action:

Anne: "I feel like there's nothing between us. You treat me like I don't exist. Here I slave away all day at work and you never help with anything. What's the matter with you?"

Peter: "Anne, I understand you're frustrated and maybe I'm not helping you out much. I've been putting in a lot of overtime lately and I didn't realize that maybe I wasn't paying as much attention to our relationship as I should. Let's talk about this and see what we can understand."

Anne: "I don't want to talk. I just want you to think about me once in a while."

Peter: "You don't have to talk. Let me do the talking. I know you've been working hard and you must be tired. Why don't you just sit down here beside me for a while and I'll rub your neck. How's that?"

Anne: "That feels great. How come you're being so nice to me when I've been shouting at you and picking on you?"

Peter: "Well, I just figured out that you're probably right that we haven't been taking care of each other lately. If this feels good to you then it's great for me. I know how tired I am and you must be even more tired. I think you've been working too hard lately."

Anne: "It sure is hard to argue with you when you're being so nice. Peter, I really appreciate that you didn't fight with me even though I sure tried to pick one."

Peter: "I know. I don't want to argue. I just want us to understand each other and work through this together. Let's go out for fast food and talk about how we can share the work around the house and see more of each other. What do you think?"

Anne: "I think you're a sweetheart; a kind one at that."

Peter: "Thank you."

Anne started with fighting and hurtful words out of habit. Peter made the choice to break their old habit of fighting by using the techniques of paraphrasing, clarification, and feedback to reach understanding. What's more, he spoke with kindness in his words and voice. Peter knew he was taking some risk but he decided that he'd give this gift of kindness. Anne felt his kindness and felt safe enough to respond positively. The fight that Anne was ready for never happened and the conversation took a positive direction to bring them closer together rather than farther apart. It may not happen this quickly for you the first time but, with practice, it can.

What a great time to avoid a fight, when you're tired and overworked. It's also the easiest time to argue because self-defense is a natural instinct. Someone says something that you don't like and your self-defense instincts kick in without even thinking. Oops, there you go toward trouble. You can do something different, however, if you can just take a moment out to think. Your thinking self can hold onto your feelings for a moment and make a judgment about what you should do. Should you fight or take flight in the normal self-defense mode or should you not take either route? If you can rationally decide that you'll work through the moment without escalation, you then have another choice and that's to think about how you're going to respond. When you're thinking, you have the further choice of responding with kindness, respect and understanding. That's a powerful choice. That choice can help to bring friends and lovers together as partners. That choice can cast out weeds and cause your flowers to grow without thorns.

Write down your answers to the following questions and use them to help you put more kindness into your relationships:

1. How do feelings get hurt in your relationship?

2. How do you think that you might change that?

Pressures against kindness:

As you saw in the prior example, Anne's frustration over Peter's lack of attention to her had built up and she exploded. Peter was tired from his overtime and in the past would have probably just responded with his own anger and frustration. In this case, however, Peter chose to seek understanding and to validate Anne's feelings. The choice was powerful for both of them. The result was a closer union rather than a fight.

One difference this time was that both Peter and Anne knew they were both under a lot of pressure. It's helpful to be aware of some of the common pressures that work against kindness. The following is a list of nine pressures that may interfere.

1. Ignorance of what is right.
2. Habit.
3. Tiredness.
4. Fear.
5. Time.

6. Anger or frustration for any reason.
7. Laziness.
8. Revenge for past disagreements.
9. Contempt or a lack of respect.

It may be easier to change behaviors that are rooted in those causes higher on the list than it is to deal with revenge, contempt, or a lack of respect. As long as you start the journey of change, you have the opportunity to reach your destination. Revitalization may be found in the use of courtesy and apology as well as the other skills and guidelines.

Courtesy

Courtesy, or why you should still say "please" and "thank you" when you don't feel you have to.

Happily married couples that we know practice simple courtesy to help keep their love alive. They say "please" and "thank you" as though the queen were present and keeping score. They don't do it out of obligation but they do it out of a true appreciation for their partner. The spoken word is powerful. When you say "thank you" you should feel it and if you say it enough, you should feel it even more.

We've talked to people who are glad to be rid of the obligation of courtesy that their parents taught them as children. They believe they are casting off the chains of their childhood/adolescent obligation. The problem is that they forgot there's a good reason for courtesy. Simply, it makes us all feel good when we do it. Exchanging courtesy is a simple way to celebrate your love.

Here are seven simple ways to be courteous:

1. Say "Please" when you ask for something.

2. Say "Thank you" when you receive something.

3. Speak with respect and kindness.

4. Acknowledge other people for their value.

5. Listen for understanding. Don't interrupt.

6. Use a positive tone in your communication.

7. Remember the good times and talk about them. Put the bad times aside and don't dwell on them.

Chivalry isn't dead. It has been wounded and it has been modernized. Originally the change was to acknowledge the equality of women. But that doesn't mean that you can't hold the door for your partner or extend other simple courtesies. Whoever has the free hand can hold the door but in other cases, men, the women just love it when you acknowledge them with such courtesy. All it takes is practice.

At the same time, don't forget to be kind to yourself. Think well of yourself and don't be harsh in your judgments. Do the best you can and move on. Everyone has things about themselves that they want to change but no one should be so judgmental that their self-esteem is dragged in the mud. The stronger your own self-esteem becomes, the more able you are to communicate well and to love. Be kind enough to forgive yourself for the past and go forward in a positive way. Remember you did the best you could with the knowledge you had at the time.

The Power of Apology

"I'm sorry" may be the most difficult words to say but they are some of the most important and powerful words in a lover's vocabulary. It's unfortunate that society teaches us to see these words as submissive and weak. They are truly words well spoken and, coupled with the power of understanding, respect, consideration and kindness, they clearly show love.

We typically don't apologize enough. Perhaps we have all seen too many types of macho movies where the only apologies made come at the point of a knife or the barrel of a gun and in submission. Perhaps we have all heard too many misdirected love songs or movie lines which speak of apology as unnecessary for true lovers. Perhaps we resent having been told to apologize by our parents. Perhaps we just aren't aware of the value and importance of well-spoken words of apology. Or perhaps we just don't know how. Both you and the recipient will be enriched by a well-meaning apology. It is a gift.

Here are three simple guidelines to making an apology:

1. It must be honest. Any lack of sincerity will show through and the apology may be seen as a negative rather than a positive. You must be comfortable with your words and intent. It should be respectful but not subservient.

2. It should be timely. The sooner the better but better late than never. If the apology is late, say so.

3. The apology should be appropriate. Don't apologize for something trivial just to divert the conversation.

In following these guidelines, you are actually seeking understanding of your own position as well as that of your partner. This leads to the gift of validation.

The willingness and ability to make an apology is one of the hallmarks of the strength of the individual as well as the relationship. You're not necessarily accustomed to saying "I'm sorry" or offering other apologies to those you love, so you may need to practice. Let's follow a conversation with Anne and Peter to see how apologies can save the day.

Anne: "Look Peter, I'm sick and tired of having to pick up your clothes around here. You told me yesterday that you'd do your share and now you aren't." (thinking: What does he think I am, his mother or his maid? I don't want to be either. I knew I couldn't trust him to keep his word about helping out.)

Peter: "Anne, I'm sorry. I forgot. I just -- "

Anne: "What do you mean you're sorry? I've heard that before from you and nothing changed." (thinking: Here we go again. Another fight.)

Peter: "Anne, I'm sorry. I truly did forget because I'm not in the habit yet. Are you thinking that I'm falling back into my old habits and we're going to start fighting over everything again?" (thinking: I blew it this time but I hope Anne understands. It takes time and practice to work these things out. I think we're learning the hard way.)

Anne: "Oh my, now I'm sorry too. I didn't take the time to think that even a simple change is hard for both of us. I thought that when you didn't pick up your clothes you were being disrespectful and that you didn't care about me or our relationship."

Peter: "Thanks for sharing your concerns with me. I just forgot to do what I said I was going to do. I love and respect you more and more each day as our understanding grows deeper.

I'll admit I had to bite my tongue and hold back when you challenged me. Old habits die hard."

Anne: "I'm so glad that we're getting to know each other better. We seem to fight less and talk more these days. I love you."

Peter: "I love you, too."

Here are some examples of how to make apologies in various circumstances without sacrificing yourself.

Misunderstandings:

- "I'm sorry. I'm not sure that I understand what you're saying. Could you please help me?"

- "I think something is wrong here and I'm not sure what it is. How can we sort this out?"

- "Did I misunderstand? I'm sorry if I did and I'd appreciate it if you would help me understand."

Mistakes:

- "I think I made a mistake. I'm sorry, would you please help me to correct this before we go on?"

- "I feel that you think I made a mistake. If that's correct, I'm sorry and would like to understand so that we can sort this out."

- "I really made a mistake and I want to talk to you about it before you find out from someone else. First of all, please know that it was an honest mistake and I'm sorry about it. I hope that you can understand and forgive me. Now let me tell you what happened."

Anger:

- "I'm sorry. I'm not mad at you. I'm upset about the kids. I just need to cool down a bit. "

- "I had a tough day at work and I'm sorry that I took it out on you by yelling. Please forgive me."

- "There I go again getting angry when I shouldn't. Please accept my apology and give me a chance to get my emotions back into balance."

When you've hurt your partner's feelings:

- "I'm sorry I said those things. I might have hurt your feelings. I spoke in anger and that's not how I feel about you. Please forgive me. I do love you and promise to work on how I say things."

- "How can I demonstrate my sincere concern for your feelings? Please remember that I have the highest respect for you even if that might not be obvious in what I've said and done. Please help me understand."

Write down your answers to the following questions and use them to help you and your partner be kind to each other:

1. What are the pressures that work against kindness in your relationship?
2. What positive steps might you take toward creating more kindness in light of what you've just learned?

SUMMARY:

- Kindness is contagious. Try it in your thoughts, and in your conversations. You'll be pleased.

- Kindness is a gift that you can give at any time. You'll find that you're kinder and have a better understanding of yourself and your partner. This will make it easier to be honest and to love. Honesty is a powerful force when directed by kindness.

- Be courteous to each other.

- Practice the power of a sincere apology.

You can do anything together if you do it with shared kindness. With kindness your dreams can become reality and your life rich with love.

Chapter Nine : Honesty

Honesty leads all of us through life. You either embrace it fully and prosper or deny it with deceit and always check your back to see if the truth has caught up with you. It may not be clear why people must so often work hard to learn to be honest. You must understand, however, that without honesty, your relationship will soon wither and die as your garden is choked with weeds. Honesty is an essential part of positive and loving communication.

Honesty is a principle and communication is one of its key representations. Honesty may be one of the most difficult choices you have to make in life. You may struggle with the choice at a young age and then live with it. Life constantly challenges you to make choices and, while it may not be easy to stay the course, it is possible.

This raises the following important questions to which we offer some answers:

What is honesty? Honesty, according to the dictionary, signifies the quality of being upright in principle and action. Honesty implies truthfulness, fairness in dealing with others, and refusal to engage in fraud, deceit, or falsity. Honesty also implies that you face reality and not avoid an issue/topic.

Why does honesty matter in loving communication? Honesty is important in general and it's vital to a loving relationship because it establishes trust, the foundation for intimacy.

- A committed relationship, especially marriage, relies on trust. When you commit to your partner, you're putting your faith in his/her commitment to guard and protect your very soul which you are sharing with him/her. You've probably shown more of your vulnerable inner-self to your partner than anyone else in your life. This is a tremendous act of faith that occurs only at great expense.

- Understanding lies within the truthful facts. Understanding is key to loving and positive intimacy.

- Honesty is one of the primary principles that represent goodness in people. Love prospers in goodness.

- Practically, you must work together for your life to function smoothly. You expect and need to know what is important in each other's lives so that you can maintain harmony.

This means that any loss of trust is a potential assault on the relationship and yourself as individuals. Even the simplest untruth or perception of a lie can be devastating. If you cannot trust each other to tell the truth about something as simple as where you were or how you spent some money, how can you trust that you both love each other? It may not be easy.

What are the elements of honest communication? Honesty is more than just telling the truth and not telling a lie. Here are five elements of honest communication.

1. Honesty contains understanding. If you speak with an understanding of your true feelings and motivations, you're more likely to be able to speak the truth. If you understand your partner and talk in a way that will help him/her to understand, you're more able to reach the truth together.

2. Honesty involves kindness and respect. Positive, loving communication is founded on that combination because it helps to keep the heart in your relationship. Being honest doesn't necessarily mean that all of the details of the truth have to be told. Some details are best left in the past. If

your motive in telling is kind rather than hurtful then you'll know what to say.

3. Timing is important to honesty. Something left unsaid at the right time or said at the wrong time can be seen as a lie. Withholding important information intentionally may have the same impact as not telling the truth.

4. Intent is a critical element to honesty. Telling an untruth without intent to deceive may be just a mistake or a misunderstanding and not a lie. It's helpful to seek understanding before rushing to judgment.

5. Trust is earned. Others judge you on how they perceive you. They filter their observation of your words and behavior and make judgments on whether or not they will trust you. You must be consistently honest in everything you do and say to establish and preserve the trust that your partner and the rest of the world share with you.

The best way to remember all of this is to accept honesty as an integral part of your life. Help yourself and your partner to accept truth and to work through the inevitable mistakes and misunderstandings to reach the goal of a shared trust in your relationship. If you have this now, congratulations. The following will help you to solidify what you have. For those who are still searching, it will help you find what you need for a trusting relationship.

Communicating with honesty.

It seems that you can get yourself into deep trouble sometimes by just saying what's on your mind at the time. And at other times, when you bite your tongue and wait, you get frustrated or bitter about not being able to say what's on your mind. In an intimate, understanding, and loving relationship you quite often have a sense of what to say, when. That's a combination of practice and the sensitive understanding of your partner. This is something you should consider more often. Here are three ways to build honesty into communication:

1. Make the conscious choice to work toward being more honest.
   - Practice thinking about how you'll say what you may have previously avoided or lied about. Use the guidelines for positive communication. Once you're comfortable with the tone of your new conversation, give it a try. Take one small step at a time as you build confidence.

2. Take an inventory of past dishonesty within the relationship and put it behind you so that the baggage doesn't weigh you down.
   - Forgiveness is very powerful. Start by forgiving yourself and then your partner.
   - Deal with the dishonesty openly with your partner. This may be difficult but it can also be very healing and helpful in building new trust and understanding.

3. Look for patterns in your communication when you feel uncomfortable about not sharing what you're truly feeling. What aren't you saying that you feel you should?
   - If you understand what you're holding back, practice talking about it in your mind and then share it with your partner, one piece at a time, when you think the time is right. Use your improved sense of timing so you don't ambush him/her.
   - If you don't fully understand what is making you feel uncomfortable, tell your partner when and

what you're feeling and ask for his/her help in understanding. This may be difficult but when you do it in a positive way you'll experience an even greater intimacy in the relationship.

Let's join our couple, Anne and Peter, mid-argument as they struggle with some issues of honesty and trust.

Anne: "Okay, I'll do whatever you want. I'll take the chair back to the store and get my money back. I'm tired of fighting about money. You win. Now just leave me alone." (thinking: I don't know how I can ever win in this relationship. He doesn't trust me and yet he buys things all the time without talking to me. We talk about sharing the responsibilities and we both work hard to make ends meet but when it comes to making decisions about how to spend money, he just doesn't think I'm smart enough.)

Peter: "Why do we always have to end up fighting over money. I thought that we agreed to share these major purchase decisions. I love you." (thinking: What's wrong here? We both work hard and we say we're going to agree on major purchases and yet she doesn't trust me enough to talk about it.)

Anne: "Look, just leave me alone. You're the one who buys things without asking me and then I'm the one who gets yelled at. You spent more money last week than I spent all month and never said a word to me. It's not fair and I don't have to take it" (thinking: He says that he loves me but he sure doesn't show it. I've got nothing to lose here. If he's going to blame me for all these problems, I'm going to let him know what I think, too.)

Peter: "That's not true. I give up. I'm out of here." (thinking: I didn't cheat on our communication agreement.

It's like talking to a wall. I get no respect around here. Some wife she is.)

Anne: "Don't hurry back." (thinking: It's like talking to a wall. I get no respect around here. Some husband he is.)

This sounds like two separate people fighting to retain their sense of identity in a relationship that just might not last long at the rate it's going. What happened? To begin with, Anne and Peter forgot to use the communication guidelines and then they went further, with a lack of honesty. Anne forgot or neglected to involve Peter in the decision to buy the chair as they'd agreed. She was retaliating for Peter purchasing things the week prior without involving her. Neither Anne nor Peter was honest, since their thoughts were different from their words. The end result was the predictable assault on each other with an eventual retreat that left no resolution of the underlying problems.

Let's have Anne and Peter try again, in the same disagreement but this time using the Fair Exchange Process and with a greater awareness of the need for honesty.

Anne: "Peter, I need a time-out here. I'm feeling some feelings that I don't like and I'd like to calm down a bit and then come back together again in fifteen minutes to see if we can work through this together. Is that okay with you?"

Peter: "Yeah. I'm afraid I'm losing my temper."

15 minutes later: Anne: "Peter, I've been thinking about it and I feel that my independence is at stake here. I may be reacting to my feeling that you broke our agreement to talk about major purchases together when you bought all of those things last week. How can we trust each other when we do things like this?"

Peter: "Anne, am I correct in understanding that you think I broke our agreement last week and that made it all right for you to not worry about the agreement now? Are you also feeling that our trust is on the line? Is there anything more?"

Anne: "You got that right but I also feel we're not listening to each other sometimes and it really frustrates me."

Peter: "So you get frustrated when you don't think I understand what you're saying and you think that I'm not doing what we agreed to. Is that right?"

Anne: "Yes. Now can you help me understand why I should listen to what you have to say about this chair?"

Peter: "First of all, I'm sorry about last week. I really thought I was following our agreement since the things I bought were for the house and the car. Now that I think about it, I did spend more money than I agreed to. I really should have talked to you and I'm sorry that I didn't. I'm sorry that I hurt you and hope you'll forgive me. It's hard to change my old habits and I sometimes need a bit of help."

Anne: "I accept your apology. It's not right for either of us to break our agreements but I understand what happened now. Now let's talk about the chair. I bought the chair to show you that I'm a part of this relationship, too. What's fair for you is fair for me. Can you understand that?"

Peter: "Yes, I understand. We shouldn't meet bad deeds with bad deeds, however. That just makes it easier to fight. What do we do now?"

Anne: "You're right. I'm sorry, too. I really do want the chair for the living room but I'll take it back today and we can wait if that's what we need to do to stay on our budget. Do you think that we can try and be more honest with each other in the future to avoid these problems? I do love you."

Now this sounds like two separate people working *together* to build trust and understanding in a relationship that has a future. What happened? Anne recognized that she wasn't being honest with her own thoughts and feelings and asked for a time-out to sort things out. She then asked Peter to help her understand the situation. Peter used good communication skills to help them both reach understanding. They both used their skills and the guidelines to work through a problem that would have previously left them feeling alone and bitter. They chose this time to take a positive approach and to plant flowers instead of weeds.

Think about a recent argument you've had and consider which of these two patterns your argument followed. Do your arguments tend to escalate and deteriorate to bad feelings or end with a shared good feeling that you've accomplished something? If you find that your arguments are hurtful for both -- based on what is said as well as what is unsaid -- you may choose to try to be more honest with yourself and with your partner about the things that are important for both of you to know. Practice in your mind and then practice with your partner.

Shattered Trust

Sometimes couples find, as they work on their communication skills, that they reach a crossroads that they may not have wanted to face before. As you become more aware of yourself and more aware of how a positive relationship should function, you may realize that you're feeling hopeless about where you are. Trust is gone and it's not clear how it can be regained. Communicating more clearly with yourself and your partner will help you overcome the first difficulty in understanding what your reality is. You may not like that reality but at least you now have a choice.

If trust has been shattered by infidelity, harsh and hurtful words or a pattern of deceit or repression, the road to healing will be difficult. The garden has gone to weed and you, the gardeners, may have given up. Some of the choices you may make at this crossroads include the following:

1. Ignore the problem and continue with the status quo by conscious choice.
2. Make the choice to quit and leave the relationship.
3. Make the choice to work on the rebuilding of trust together.
   - You may try to do this on your own with books and other similar resources.
   - You may find it useful to have a professional third party, such as clergy or professional counselors, to help you.

Without having an understanding of your personal situation, we cannot prescribe the path that you should take. We do, however, recommend that you choose not to maintain an abusive relationship. If you're in an abusive relationship and find that you cannot change the pattern on your own, we recommend that you consult with the crisis center and/or other resources that are listed in the phone book. The domestic violence hot line is 1-800-942-6906. They can help guide you.

Positive outcomes can be found in change. Troubled relationships can be fixed or new relationships can be created when old ones are just not meant to be. **The first step is taken**

when you're honest with yourself about where you are in your relationship and what it means to you.

SUMMARY:

You must strive to be honest with yourself and to understand what is driving you. Sometimes it is hard to face bitter feelings such as hurt and disappointment. You may have a difficult enough time dealing with them much less understanding them. It's no surprise then that they sometimes express themselves not in rational words, but in irrational and hurtful ways. Honest understanding can only help.

- You can remember to be honest by holding it as a principle that you'll live up to at all times.

- Honesty includes saying the right thing at the right time.

- Forgiveness is a powerful way to put the past behind you so you can create a new future.

- If you have the help of your partner, the mutual understanding will light the path for you to take.

- Honesty establishes trust, the foundation of intimacy.

- Work on understanding why you don't say what you feel and help your partner understand.

- If trust has been shattered, make a positive, conscious choice to resolve the issue.

Honesty will help your relationship garden grow. Forgive your pasts and create a new future together based on honesty, commitment and trust.

Chapter Ten : Respect

True love can only exist with self respect and respect for each other. This last guideline (respect) is possible only when the first three (understanding, kindness, honesty) are followed. When you act with the intent of being respectful of your partner at all times, you are strengthening your love. What you say and how you say it can be music to your love; inviting good communication. Or the words can be threatening and cause your partner to be defensive and stop communication.

Criticism is often a symptom of a lack of respect. Positive communication is a strong builder of relationships while criticism, we believe, is a primary destroyer. Criticism, according to the dictionary, is the act of making judgments; the act of finding fault; censuring; disapproval. This is all very negative and, try as you might, you will usually perceive criticism as a negative assault on your person. You get way too much criticism from the outside world: from parents, bosses, family members, the media, etc. Your loving relationship is the one part of your life that should be safe and free from criticism.

Criticism causes doubt that can quickly grow like weeds in your garden. It's so much better to never plant those negative thoughts than to have to weed them out later.

Sometimes it's easier to show respect to a stranger than it is to show respect to your lover. Why is that? Why do you have so much trouble, at times, being respectful to others, even your partner? The basic reason is most likely that you mistakenly expect the power of love to make all things right. You don't have to take the trouble to be respectful because it's part of the package that comes with love. You may even feel like overlooking many of the problems you have when you're still caught in the wonderful anesthesia of passion. Once passion fades a bit, you then feel the problems. One problem may be a lack of respect in the way that you treat each other. Some of the ways that respect is never established, lost or abused in relationships include the following:

1. Habits are established based on improper role models. They are all around.
2. Due care and maintenance of respect isn't shown.
3. Criticism is a part of the relationship behaviors.
4. One or both of the partners has low self-esteem and low self-respect.
5. Problems are taken and handled personally rather than as problems. Assaults on each other tend to result with an obvious lack of respect.
6. Kindness is forgotten.
7. Trust is lost or abused.
8. Jealousies get in the way.
9. Outside parties inflict their standards or opinions on the relationship.
10. Boundaries and expectations aren't set and agreed to by the couple.

The world is full of too many such examples that challenge respect. Television programming, for example, is full of bad examples.

The most influential example that you may have had in life, however, is the one provided by your parents. Whether you were conscious of it or not, you were aware of how your mother and father or other caretakers communicated and treated each other as you were growing up. If respect was an obvious part of their relationship, then you probably learned some positive skills concerning how to treat your partner with respect. On the other hand, if there was a lack of respect or it wasn't obvious that your parents worked at maintaining respect for each other, you may have either learned the wrong lesson or an insufficient lesson. Even with good lessons, you must remember that you and your partner aren't the same people you learned from. **It's now up to you to create your own respectful relationship together.**

You can make the choice to put the respect back into yourself and your relationship. There are a number of ways to take action right now. You have problems. Everyone does. That's life. So how can you communicate when you think that what you have to say is a difficult topic or might be seen as negative by the other person? **You can make a discussion of such hot topics much easier just by rephrasing "you" statements into "I" or "we" statements.** This removes the finger pointing and implication of blame. The words are less offensive and the response should be less defensive. As you know, once you're on the defensive, understanding is much harder to obtain. That's also true for your partner. You'll want to avoid defensive situations in the first place.

<u>Speaking with respect</u>

Here are some examples of how to speak with more respect and less criticism:

Before: *"You're* the problem. It's *your* fault. I want *you* to fix it now."

Rephrased: "What can *we* do together to solve this problem? *I'm* willing to do the following ...."

How you say things really matters.

Before: *"You* never listen to me."

Rephrased: *"I'd* like *us* to spend some time together to better understand each other."

Before: *"You* never do anything to help around the house."

Rephrased: "How can *we* share the chores so that neither of us feels overburdened?"

Before: *"You* never tell me you love me."

Rephrased: *"I* love you and *I* feel so good when *I* hear you say 'I love you.' Could you say it more often?"

Before: *"You* never make love to me or show me any affection."

Rephrased: *"I* hope you feel as good as *I* do when we're affectionate. In what ways might *we* share that more often?"

Before: "Stop nagging me. Get off my back."

Rephrased: *"I* think that *we'd* both feel better if *we* exchanged more compliments and less criticism. *I'll* do my part by being kinder."

Before: *"You* always spend too much. *You* didn't need that new suit and we can't afford it."

Rephrased now: *"I* realize that it's very important for you to feel good about the way you look. *I* think you wear your clothes very well. Could *we* talk now or would it be better in an hour?

Continued later: *"I'm* personally concerned about how we can balance the budget to make ends meet and still get some of the nice things that you want. *I'd* appreciate it if you'd help me look over our budget to see if *we're* spending our money in ways that *we're* both comfortable with."

Before: *"Your* mother is always sticking her nose in our business. *You* need to tell her to leave us alone."

Rephrased: "Now that *we're* trying to establish *our* own family and our own way of living, *I* think we should be careful not to let any of our parents influence us too much. *I* believe they're looking out for our best interest but they really don't need to run our lives for us. *I* trust you and *me* to do that just fine. Maybe *we* should set some boundaries so *we* can be more independent. *We* both love our parents and I'm sure they'll understand. What do you think?"

In these examples the rephrasing has taken away the finger pointing and criticism and gives respect to the listener. Take personal ownership of the feelings and opinions by using "I" instead of "you" in most cases. "I" am now responsible and in a position to take action as well. "I" am not forcing all of the guilt, blame or responsibility onto "you." Notice how this also makes it easier to explain both your feelings and thoughts behind the position. These details make it much easier for both you and your partner to understand. **The absolute statements like "always" and "never" were removed.** The difficult questions relating to money and in-laws were further rephrased to include some positive suggestions to help each partner think about the problem or the question in a productive way.

Remember that when you're bringing up hot topics, you may have had much more time to get your thoughts together. Your partner may be coming in cold and even soft words can seem to be very hard. Give yourself time to understand and take the time and effort to ease your partner into the subject and help him/her to understand as well as you do.

Listening with respect: Ignoring someone is a sure way to show a lack of respect. It says that the person doesn't even care enough to pay attention. If you have ever been given the "cold shoulder," you probably felt that you weren't respected.

It's important for you and your partner to agree that you will at least listen to each other. This is why the first guideline is Understanding. Your active pursuit of understanding shows that you care. Again, you don't always have to agree. In fact, if you and your partner both feel that you understand and respect each other, whatever decision you reach will be much, much easier to accept. Consider these examples. Which do you prefer?

> Before: "No, I don't care what you think. I won't do it."

> Rephrased: "I understand your opinion and you have made some good points. I'd feel more comfortable if we don't do that. I hope you understand."

> Before: "Don't bother me. Do what you want. You always do anyway."

> Rephrased: "I'm really tired and stressed out. I might not be able to listen to you as well as you'd like right now. Could we talk about this in an hour or so after I get some aspirin?

Kindness and respect: People who respect each other are polite and don't call each other names or talk about them in a demeaning way. They don't even pretend to joke about their partner. Such "put down" comments are a sure sign that there is something wrong in the relationship. The person who makes the "put down" doesn't respect you. If you put up with it, you may not respect yourself either.

Teenagers may get into the habit of playfully abusing each other with words. There's no room, however, for verbal abuse, even in "fun" in a loving relationship.

If you are saying disrespectful things, stop. If your partner is being unkind and disrespectful, point it out to them using "I" statements telling them what you are observing and what you feel or think about it. Then, kindly and respectfully, ask them to stop. Set your boundaries. Then, work on your communication so you can strengthen your relationship and respect.

Respect and honesty: Where there is honesty, trust can exist. Where there is trust, respect is possible. You can strengthen your relationship with honesty, trust and respect.

If you feel a lack of trust, practice the recommendations in Chapter 9 on "Honesty." You and your partner, working together, can develop and earn mutual trust and respect. Even on your own you can strengthen your self-trust and self-respect.

SUMMARY:

In order for a relationship to be ideal and lasting each person must be **respectful** toward the other. "Respectful," according to Webster's, means: to feel or show honor or esteem for; hold in high regard; to consider or treat with deference or dutiful regard.

Put these words to practice in your conversations, thoughts and actions:

R - respectful, responsible, reassure
E - educate, encourage, evolve
S - sincere, sympathetic, support
P - praise, practice, patience
E - encouragement, enjoyment, enthusiasm
C - communicate, cuddle, compliment
T - truth, trust, tenderness
F - faithfulness, fulfillment, fun
U - understand, unite, uplift
L - listen, learn, love, laugh

You have the choice. The benefits will be yours.

Chapter Eleven : Communicating Under Stress

Why does it seem that the more you need to talk, the harder it is to do so? And why is it that when you do talk under stress, the words sometimes become louder and louder until no one can hear what's being said? The answer is that the higher and more intense the emotions are and the more difficult the issue is, the harder it is to gain understanding. You are caught in your own self-preservation mode, fighting for yourself, and you may not be able hear or see each other as partners on the same team. Those who are afraid for their relationship or of each other are trapped and under pressure. On the other hand, partners who have learned to communicate well can rise above these problems. They can talk to each other with the confidence that they can, as a team, work through the problem to resolution. This is a true measure of respect, as well as a positive element of any good and loving relationship.

When times are hard, hard work is probably required to make sure that you and your partner both communicate for understanding. Don't be so distracted by the problem that you forget who you two are. You are on the same team, working together in a loving way to make the best life for each other and your family. Just like in sports, people who are on the same team cooperate with each other to solve problems. Teammates work together. Their individual contributions are important but it's the combination that allows them to win. Everyone plays by the rules of good sportsmanship. The sports team model offers some good lessons for you to follow. Ask your partner to be your teammate.

While the following chapter on "How to Succeed" will cover this in more detail, here are seven powerful tips to use when you are under stress.

1. Try to reduce your emotional level before you talk to your partner. Your partner, in a natural response, will tend to react to and pick up the stress that you feel. Even if he/she isn't stressed to begin with, he/she will feel yours and act the same way you are acting. Take a time-out if you feel your emotional stress level rising too high again.

2. If you are unable to calm down enough to be sure your emotions don't get in the way, tell your partner that you're upset, angry, frustrated, or whatever and why. Also tell him/her that it's *your* feeling and that *you* take responsibility for it. It helps if you can reassure your partner that it's not his/her fault that you feel this way. Ask for his/her help in listening and understanding what you have to say.

3. You might wish to call a time-out by saying, "I see that we are getting into a fight and we don't want to do that. I suggest we take some time-out to calm down and discuss the issue in thirty minutes or so when/if we are both ready."

4. Practice with small points of concern and address them quickly and positively. For example, if you are arguing or debating about where to eat and it truly doesn't matter to you, tell your partner that your desire is to spend quality time together and not to argue over where to eat. Then accept his/her decision gracefully.

5. If the situation is too tense for you to speak in a positive way, write a short note to your partner using some of the positive words and phrases we covered earlier.

6. Acknowledge that you understand or wish to better understand your partner's point of view. Work toward that understanding. Ask your partner to consider your point of view and to seek an acceptable solution.

7. Try the speaker - listener technique for speaking. Take turns using "the floor" so you don't interrupt each other and do have a chance to listen and understand.

What creates stress in a relationship?

The presence of stress doesn't indicate that there's an absence of love. Even loving relationships will have some level of stress and tension. This tension comes from the natural desire of each partner to be fulfilled as an individual. An individual's first desire in life is to be fulfilled as a person and the second desire is to attain fulfillment with another. This paradox naturally leads to some need for accommodation in the relationship. How well you handle this tension and other differences has a real impact on how you feel about yourself and your relationship. The following is a simple assessment of stress. Please complete it now. Then we'll discuss some of the causes and approaches for reducing stress.

Here are some of the feelings that you may experience in everyday life, but seem so difficult to deal with in a relationship. <u>Place one of the following numbers by each feeling to indicate how often you feel these feelings in your relationship</u>.

1 = never, 2 = rarely, 3 = sometimes, 4 = often, 5 = very often.

1. Fear   _____
2. Tiredness/exhaustion   _____
3. Anger   _____
4. Annoyance   _____
5. Exasperation   _____
6. Discontent   _____
7. Bitterness   _____
8. Concern   _____

9. Hate   _____
10. Jealousy   _____
11. Selfishness   _____
12. Loneliness   _____
13. Overwhelmed   _____
14. Confusion   _____
15. Sadness   _____

TOTAL   _____ add up the numbers

Ratings: The following scores indicate how much stress you might have in your relationship.

> 15 - 30   low stress; pretty calm
> 31 - 45   more tense than you might like
> 46 - 75   it's time to change for the better

None of these feelings is unnatural, although having a lot of them often would indicate a troubled and negative situation. You can expect to feel them at times in your life as a natural part of living. Your work or activities outside of your home life may bring on these feelings, but when you bring them home, you're sharing them with your partner whether you know it or not. Balancing these feelings with the positive is sometimes a challenge. You don't want to have them in a loving relationship so you either don't acknowledge them or you don't know how to deal with them with your lover. Yes, it's hard to deal with difficult situations in a positive and loving way with your lover but you can do it if you communicate with each other in a constructive way.

Causes of Stress:

Here are ten common causes for stress in relationships and some actions you can take to reduce the impact of stress:

1. Poor communication: This is a primary cause for stress. It's also implicated as a cause to some extent in almost every broken relationship. Don't feel badly. You just weren't taught how to communicate well under most circumstances. And you probably weren't taught how to communicate with your lover. Until you and your partner work through the blocks and barriers to communication and establish your own ground rules for communication, you can expect to have some level of ongoing stress.

This book is designed to help you reduce this stress and to create loving and positive communications. You can learn how to handle both the problems and opportunities of life.

2. The natural tension of intimacy: The closer you are to someone else, the more opportunity you have for tension. It's a real thrill to get to know someone for the first time but after living together for a while, those cute behaviors might become annoying. You may feel closed in or smothered by your partner.

Living closely with someone else and sharing life takes practice. Practicing loving communication will help.

Have your own space and time so you can relax from the closeness. As much as you want to be together, you still need some time to yourself. You each need to enjoy your own interests.

3. The Pursuit/Withdrawal Cycle: Women, in general, have a natural tendency to try to talk right away about what is important to them. Talking makes them feel better even when the issue may be emotional. Women will pursue the conversation. Men, on the other hand, have a natural survival tendency to withdraw from conflict. That masculine tendency

kicks in even when a woman wants to talk about an emotional issue. The pursuit/withdrawal cycle goes like this: the woman approaches the man to talk, the man withdraws (He says "I don't want to talk about it now." He needs time to get accustomed to the idea.), the woman feels abandoned and approaches more vigorously (She says "We need to talk about this now."), the man withdraws even further (He says "Leave me alone.") and before either of them know it, they are both hurt and fighting.

The use of appointments of agreed time, duration and subject is a great way to break this destructive downward spiral. This gives the man a chance to think about the subject and prepare.

**Stress levels will stay lower when you
don't ambush your partner.**

4. <u>Lack of understanding</u>: If you feel that you're not appreciated for who you are, it's difficult to love yourself and others. If it seems as though your partner doesn't agree with whatever you have to say, you may see it as an attack on yourself even though it probably isn't.

Seeking to understand your partner while communicating with honesty, kindness, and respect can go a long way toward establishing mutual understanding.

It sometimes helps to express your feelings that you might not be understood on a point and ask to work together to reach understanding. Also see the practice dialogues and recommendations in the next chapter " How to Succeed."

5. <u>Concern for self</u>: You walk a delicate balance between self-esteem and selfishness through much of your life. When you're in a relationship, this balance is further complicated by the balance between "I" and "We." Any lack of self-worth and

identity (I) will be felt personally and may reflect in the relationship (we) in a number of ways, including a feeling that there's insufficient understanding and connection between you and your partner. You might feel that your partner is too judgmental and won't let you be yourself. You might see your partner as you might have seen your parents or other authority figures and rebel to assert your independence. At the same time you are each trying to reaffirm yourself and validate your worth as individuals.

Whatever the cause of the concern for yourself, the practice of understanding in your communication will help both you and your partner address those concerns and reaffirm your worth as individuals.

In some cases a partner lacks self-esteem and may seek to feel better by bringing the other partner to their level. Misery does love company. If you find yourself in this role, we suggest that you work on your self-esteem. *Talk to Me* will help and there are additional resources listed in the back of the book.

If your partner suffers from low self-esteem, we suggest that you work on yourself and then assist your partner with self-esteem building exercises, as well as your continual practice of the Guidelines for Loving Communication.

6. Baggage: You came into the relationship with every problem you've ever had in life. Some of them are still unresolved. Some of them you may not understand or even recognize. You and your partner will react to each other in ways that were developed as habit before you even met. Your opinions, attitudes, feelings and behaviors have already been patterned by your life. Some of these may become problems for your new relationship. You may even behave negatively when you shouldn't.

118

Seek to understand why you react the way you do. Be open to listening to what your partner and others observe. They may provide insight for you. Ask your partner to help you understand. Help him/her as well.

Start over. If for example, one of your old problems resulted in a lack of trust, start over by giving your new relationship the benefit of the doubt. Work to create a new foundation.

Treat each day as a new day. Each new day is a chance to create a better life without the problems of the past.

7. Wounded child: Teachers such as John Bradshaw and Harville Hendricks recognize that many individuals grow up with a wounded inner child struggling within. The wounded inner child is a part of us that we probably can't even see or remember. It's the hidden memory of hurts and unfulfilled needs from our childhood. That hidden inner child yearns for love and satisfaction and can influence our lives in significant ways. You can be driven to satisfy an old childhood need without even knowing why. Those unresolved wounds cloud everything that you do. You may even consciously or unconsciously choose a partner because you think they can heal those wounds.

Healing doesn't happen on its own. Take some time to consider where you are today. If you cannot understand why you are unhappy with the way you act, you might find it useful to spend some time reading or listening to Bradshaw or Hendricks. Some of their books and tapes are listed in the resource list at the back of this book.

8. History: Some of you remember every harsh word you've ever heard or misunderstanding that you've ever had in your relationship. This history can accumulate one word at a time

and get in the way of love without you ever knowing you've built a wall of defense.

Sometimes the best thing you can do is to make a fresh start. Forgiveness is marvelous as it puts the past behind you and allows you to build a new future.

Forgiveness, while it may be difficult, is truly a choice. Make that choice and go on.

Build a new history by starting fresh with yourself and your partner. This doesn't mean putting your head in the sand but it does mean that you'll make more choices about the present. Try not to let the important things in your life and your relationships just happen to you. Choose what you'll do with your life and how you'll respond. It takes practice but the fact that you're reading this book does indicate a willingness to create your own future.

9. <u>Sexuality</u>: This is the highest level of physical intimacy and it includes a strong psychic element that you may not have experienced prior to this relationship. The feelings and emotions associated with sex aren't always within your understanding or control. This exciting element of passion plays a key role in intimate relationships. How that role plays out in the long run will depend to a great extent on the overall strength of the relationship. It's not uncommon for there to be tension associated with sexuality as each partner tries to find him/herself, and the relationship, at the same time.

Patience, understanding, and positive communication are key to negotiating your relationship. If you can practice talking through the simpler things in life, you will be able to work up to this topic one step at a time.

If you feel that you've reached a block, consider stepping back to work on intimacy. Remember that sex, for women, is usually mental and emotional first, while it's usually physical first for men. Understanding can be very erotic.

10. Children: Children represent both a challenge and an opportunity in that their arrival changes your lives forever. It helps to have established good communication before your first child is born. There's no test of communication skills like trying to make major life adjustments and decisions while you're sleep-deprived by a baby. By nature, the mother and child will bond in a new love that neither have experienced before. Father will now be creating his new relationship with his child and adjusting to a wife who is now a mother. Things have changed forever.

Recognize that even change for the good is stressful and it may take a lot of communication to create a new balance and understanding in the couple's relationship. Talk about the changes and how they are affecting all of you. Make choices about how you would like these changes to be part of your relationship in the future.

Remind each other that you're both on the same team and renew your commitment to work together. Keep your loving relationship as a couple the number one priority. Show the children how a loving couple communicates and works through life together. Show them how you preserve each other's identities while creating a new and powerful joint relationship. Teach your children how to enjoy the benefits of your relationship without them coming between the two of you.

With your relationship as first priority and children second, your marriage relationship will prosper and your children will learn how to become the good parents of the future. This is a gift for all.

SUMMARY:

- Stress is a part of everyday life. Talking with your partner can help reduce relationship stress. Every little bit of stress reduction helps.

- As you use the Guidelines for Positive Communication and this information on stress you are building a foundation for deeper understanding and better cooperation.

- The guidelines can be used alone or in the context of the Couple's Fair Exchange Process which was introduced earlier. Using them will reduce your relationship stress. The combination is powerful.

- Make appointments to talk about problems. Some couples have set weekly times for problem discussions. Don't let them dominate your every waking hour. Have safe times when you can talk about everything but problems.

- Keep the common causes for stress in mind. Don't let stress come between you. Work together as a team.

Agree to keep problems in their place and to keep your conversations safe and enjoyable. When you both work as a team to understand and manage stress, you will find it much easier to talk with each other.

Chapter Twelve : How to Succeed

Success is possible. You can create positive, loving communication. It probably took time for your relationship to come to the place it is now. Or, if you're just starting a new relationship, it may take a while for you to bring it to the place that you want it to be. Like most things in life, it may take more work and time than you initially expected, but don't be discouraged. A good dose of commitment, faith and effort will go a long way even when there are weeds in the garden or bumps in the road.

We've talked about many of the positive aspects of intimacy and positive communications. You've had the chance to rate your communication skills as well as those of your partner. Hopefully, you've both done the ratings and assessments, compared them and have already begun a dialogue about the positive changes that you both can make to create more positive communication. This is a powerful act in itself and if you haven't yet completed the ratings, we suggest that you do so now.

If you choose not to have your partner complete the ratings at this time, that's okay. We understand that sometimes your partner just isn't ready to do what you are. We all come from different places and may be in different stages of our lives. If your partner doesn't want to work on communication the way you want to, maybe there's a different path that he/she can take. Whatever the case, the following information on the barriers to success and strategies for getting around them will give you the personal power to take charge of your side of the relationship. Remember that you come first as a person and that the relationship flows from both partners as individuals. When you're active in creating positive change for yourself, everyone around you will benefit.

In Chapter One, "The Loving Garden," you read about Anne and Peter struggling, as many of us do, to deal with change in themselves, their work and their relationship. You also saw them finally realizing, one at a time, that they had to make changes to adjust to all of the life events that were happening around them. They made the choice to change the way they communicated and related to one another in order to gain control of their own selves and the relationship. As they became successful for themselves and the relationship, this had a positive influence on the people around them.

<u>Who are you?</u> You have your own personality. Each of you sees yourself in your own unique way. You experience life from your own perspective and in your own style. Some people, for example, make decisions in an instant while others struggle to make the same decision over a long time. Some experience life through their feelings and emotions. Others think about everything. Some people use intuition while others use logic to explain everything. The key point is that until you understand your own style preferences and those of your partner, you may be talking past each other. Your language and timing may not be his/hers.

You may find it useful to learn more about your own personality. One way to do this is to take a personality measure. The measures are like tests, with descriptions as the outcome rather than grades. The book *Please Understand Me*, for example, has a set of measures you can take. It also provides descriptions of the various personality preferences that the measures indicate you might have. Such information can be comforting and very useful for understanding the differences and similarities that you and your partner have. See the recommended reading list for more information on the book.

Even if you choose not to use the measures, just exploring your differences with your partner can be a powerful experience. Talk about your differences, seek to understand them, and make them your allies.

Catherine and I, for example, share a love for people. Catherine is more of an extrovert personality (outgoing and comfortable with meeting new people) while I am more of an introvert (a bit shy and happy to be alone at times). It has been important for our relationship to understand this difference. Sometimes when Catherine wants to stay in a group and meet a few dozen more new people, I'm tired by the experience and ready to be alone for awhile. We understand each other and negotiate an agreement about when we will go home. We don't argue about such things. Our mutual understanding and care for each other makes the communication easy. We value our differences and respect each other for who we are. You, too, can achieve understanding and learn to accept and respect your differences.

Change

Change is difficult and even change for the better is stressful. This has been established in a number of excellent studies that show that, given enough change and stress, we even have a much higher chance of getting sick. Beyond that, most of you have some degree of concern or fear of change. It may be as simple as not wanting to have the furniture or the medicine chest rearranged, or it may be as difficult as changing the way you behave. Humans are, typically, so set in their ways that it's amazing anyone can live together, much less to do it successfully the first time. Speaking of change, what happens when you get married? If the engagement and wedding aren't enough stress, you then rush off to a honeymoon during which you're obligated to perform a fantasy vacation. You then follow this with the hugely complex task of trying to make a life together. Oh yes, you get to do this under the watchful eyes of strangers -- the in-laws and your partner's friends -- as well as the rest of the world who are judging you -- or so you think -- on every move you make. You hear them asking, "How long will they last?" or maybe they're saying "They're such a lovely couple. I'm sure they'll get along well. They'll never fight." Any way you look at it the pressure of expectation is tremendous. You, the loving newlyweds, are now thrust into the spotlight of other's, as well as your own, expectations. It may help to have dated for a long time or, as some believe, to have lived together for a while to give yourselves a chance to be confronted by some of the pressures of life before making that final commitment. But, in any case, getting married is still a significant change.

The marriage ceremony, for many people, starts a silent and important change as the honeymoon period begins its end. You and your partner now no longer feel the need to act your best to win your ideal mate. Your focus shifts from pleasing your partner to pleasing yourself in this new and permanent relationship. In some cases, during courtship, you may have focused more on pleasing your partner and less on yourself than you would want to for the long term. As your partner makes the same adjustment, you both may feel a change you don't understand or like. On top of this, passion begins to fade and the routine problems of life must be dealt with. All of this natural change can lead to strong feelings such as regret, fear, concern or even a feeling of loss for the passion of the courtship and honeymoon period. These strong feelings can make it even more difficult to communicate, to really talk heart to heart when you need it the most. Even if you and your partner didn't experience these feelings, the pressures of change are a challenge for almost anyone. The communication skills we share with you in this book will help you succeed.

Your communication skills will be tested sooner or later in your relationship. You can create positive communication skills from the start and you can repair communications that have been damaged. Don't feel bad if you don't pass the first tests as long as you're willing to study and work together for a good relationship.

Overcoming barriers:

As discussed earlier in this chapter, change can be difficult. Understanding is a powerful tool for you to use on your road to success. Let's take a look at some of the typical barriers that might get in your way and work through the solutions so that you can succeed.

You can place many of the potential barriers into five general categories:

1. Only one partner wants to try
2. History
3. Habit
4. Lack of knowledge
5. Depression or other mental conditions

Let's go through these five barrier categories one at a time to develop a better understanding of what they might mean to you and how you might be able to work around or through them successfully.

Barrier 1. Only one partner wants to try:

You know it's frustrating if you think that you're the only one really trying. Any hint of that can cause some people to quit. The first sign of this frustration is a signal that you should now figure out where you and your partner are coming from. First of all, what you currently see as a lack of commitment on your partner's part to the effort may be something else that you don't see or understand yet. First work hard for understanding. The better you understand yourself and your partner, the better off you'll be. Remember, you both shared in the circumstance that brought you to where you are today.

Some of the causes for a lack of willingness or ability to make an effort to cause a change in the relationship can be found in the following list. Sometimes it's a single event, but more often it's a pattern that has been established by an individual's history.

Failed past attempts:

How many times have you heard the statement "We've already tried it and it didn't work" so you don't want to try again? Failure can be discouraging but there are ways to succeed.

Don't do the same things over and over again and expect automatic success. Yes it's true that you have to consider the past, but you must also remember that the future is what you make it. You automatically fail if you don't try. You can succeed by reminding yourself and your partner that you do have the opportunity to make a new future by working through the past. You can agree to set the past failures aside for a moment, decide what you want the future to look like, and then work toward that future together.

Another option is to agree to do something different. Recognize that whatever you did in the past didn't work, so something new is called for. A good way to start this is to make changes in your own behavior even before you raise the subject with your partner. This advice is, in fact, useful for most of the changes that we recommend in positive communication. There's no better role model than yourself. You have the opportunity to enjoy the feeling that you're doing something positive no matter what. And you have the opportunity to catch your partner's attention in a positive way. They may see the benefits of improved communication without you even raising the subject of change. The bottom line is that you can try again with the *Talk to Me* information.

Trust is missing:

Trust is fragile. It doesn't take much to replace trust with distrust. Your own fears and concerns can be enough to damage trust even when your partner has done nothing. You can rebuild or strengthen trust one step at a time if both of you agree.

Talking about the areas where trust is weak is a good first step. Just be sure to use the Guidelines for Positive Communication. Trust comes from understanding. Remember how Anne had to learn to understand and then trust Mary in The Loving Garden (Chapter One). When Anne trusted Mary she was able to use the lessons to start communicating more honestly with her husband Peter. As Anne and Peter learned to trust themselves and each other, their communication improved, their words and actions matched their thoughts and they fell in love all over again.

Anne and Peter also stopped mind reading - guessing what each other was thinking and that alone stopped a lot of misunderstandings which were eating away at their trust. Your words, feelings and actions must match for trust to exist. That is the ultimate measure of success. You and your partner can choose to make this a priority.

Never established communications:

If you've never made the intimate connection with your partner, you now have that history to work through.

A lack of communication from the start isn't uncommon. You may never have talked about important matters together. Or, you may have only argued until someone won or you just dropped the subject rather than to talk it through.

A good way to start communication is to pick a small topic or issue that is easy. Start talking about the good times you have shared. Reminisce about them together. Discuss the good times you share now. It helps to talk about anything. Try something such as what to have for dinner or what movie to see. Use the Couple's Fair Exchange Process. Even if you are the only one using the process, you will set a positive example for your partner. Continue to practice the process in any way that you are comfortable. It may take some time for you and your partner to work up to the point where you can tackle the tough issues as a team. Remember positive, loving communication is created one word at a time.

Lack of motivation:

It takes effort to make a change. You and/or your partner may not see any benefit that will motivate you to make a change If a person truly doesn't care, however, that might be a message unto itself.

One motivated person can make a difference by working on themselves. As they change and grow the relationship will change and grow. For every action there is a reaction.

If you reach a road-block, counseling may be a good approach. You can decide what you will do as an individual and move on.

Fear:

You can be afraid of change even when you don't like what you have. Or, you may be afraid of the consequences of the intimacy that you build with effective communication. Sometimes individuals don't want to be found out. You may be afraid that if you're truly known for who you are you won't be loved.

The advice to "feel the fear and do it anyway" is a good place to start. Often when we face our fears they fall by the wayside.

Fear is very natural and quite often just understanding the source of the fear is enough to make good progress on working through it. Sharing your fears with your partner or a close friend may be enough to help you release your fear and go forward.

Barrier 2. History:

Your partner sees you in terms of your history together. What you've done and said defines who you are. Yes, we've said that people change, so relying on history is a very dangerous thing to do but look at it from your partner's point of view. Your partner is not a mind reader so he/she can only go on his/her memories of how you've acted in particular circumstances. In this way your expectations can get in the way of change. More often, however, it's the hurt, frustration or disappointment of past events that you carry around that get in the way. You may be so burdened by parts of the past that you just can't visualize change.

You have a pattern concerning your expectations of your partner. You expect them to do things in a reliable and predictable way. This is important to the relationship because very few can tolerate random and unexpected behavior from loved ones for very long. At the same time, however, those patterns can get in the way. For example, if you're accustomed to first saying "no" to any request, how long do you think it'll take for your partner to anticipate that response to everything he/she says? What would the expected response be if he/she asked you to work on the relationship? Do you think this might make it harder for them to ask the question in the first place?

What do you expect to happen when you bring up a sensitive subject that has been fought over before? Wow, talk about a time for history to get in the way. You may not even remember what the argument was about but you'll remember the aftermath: the tears, the pain, and the loneliness.

<u>We recommend you choose an old argument that you might have repeated with your partner.</u> Run through the old script and re-write it in your head or on paper. Rehearse new lines for your part until they sound or feel right to you and the outcome is a positive one that you're happy with. The next time it looks like this argument is going to start, make the choice to use the new script and work toward a positive outcome. This advice works well for almost any type of argument or misunderstanding and you'll eventually find yourself with a new set of scripts to replace your old bad habits. Even if your partner isn't in tune to what you're doing, you can have a positive influence on the outcome.

Barrier 3. Habit:

You may have wondered why some people stay in unhappy relationships when it seems obvious from the outside that it's not working. Sometimes the reason is that neither partner wants to change. They are accustomed to whatever it is that they have and forget that life can be different. A common finding with couples who can't communicate or solve their problems is that they secretly think or feel that it's the other person who can't communicate, not them. It's the other person who has the problem and they continue to think "I'm right and you are wrong." In order for a change to occur in a relationship someone needs to get off the *merry go round*. If you and your mate continue to fight and rarely solve the problems or resolve the conflicts then it's time one of you gets off the *merry go round* by no longer participating in the fights. Don't respond in the same way. Do something different.

There are many "right ways" of thinking and feeling. There are several ways to do the same thing and they can all be good and right. If you want to improve your relationship, then get off the *merry go round* and start a new day of positive, loving open communication and problem solving by practicing the following:

1. **Be responsible.** No one can *make* us feel anything. You are totally responsible for your own feelings. Learn to be less reactive to the emotional state of your partner -- you don't have to react the way they are choosing to act. Understand that they are responsible for their feelings. You can choose not to play the same old game or act in the same old way. Choose, instead, to try to understand and validate your partner's feelings. Be the example of not overreacting. Review what you might be doing that is contributing to the problem and then work on fixing *it* not your partner.

2. **Apologize.** A sincere apology goes along way in a relationship. Admit that you are part of the problem and say you are sorry. Affirm that you will start right now releasing your secret belief that you are right and your partner is wrong. Let go of that belief.

3. **Say "Thank you."** Use common courtesy words like *please* and *thank you* often. When we treat our partners with courtesy on a regular basis, he/she will respond in a positive way. **Be consistent with your courtesies.**

4. **Lighten up**. Do something with your partner that you both find fun and enjoyable. Reminisce about the days when you first met and remember the good feelings you had with your partner. Tell your partner at least three (3) things you really like about them. **Continue this practice** and sooner than later your partner will reciprocate.

Remember:

Learning anything new may seem awkward or difficult at first. Practice makes things comfortable and second nature. It's okay to feel self conscious at first trying these new behaviors. Continue using and practicing them until they become a habit. We all think our views make sense and that our complaints are reasonable and valid. **Wait until you can see things from your partner's perspective before you tell them your thoughts and feelings.** Saying something like the following to your partner helps: "Seeing things from your eyes I can understand why you feel the way you do." This statement alone validates your partner's feelings. It doesn't mean you are agreeing with them, it just validates their feelings. All of us want and need our feelings validated. Try it! It works!

If your partner doesn't choose to help you improve your communication it may be that they don't want to. They might be satisfied keeping everything just the way it is. If you want to get off the *merry go round*, and they don't, they may be telling you they don't care or that they are going to need more help than you alone can give them -- you may want to get some outside help.

Barrier 4. Lack of knowledge:

If you've read this far in *Talk to Me* you're already on your way to removing this block. Congratulations. Don't feel bad if you have never been taught how to talk with your partner. We must learn how to communicate in intimacy and under pressure with few teachers. It seems that our parents weren't taught either so they had little experience in teaching this skill to pass on to you. We are expected to learn by example. Let's face it, some of those examples are bad. On one extreme we see couples who relate so poorly that they have terrible relationships. And on the other extreme we see the Hollywood perfect couples in movies and TV shows. Nowhere do we see the real life people with their everyday joys and sorrows. We just don't have the opportunity very often to observe and learn from real people as they talk and sometimes argue their way successfully through life. We brought Peter and Anne to you here in *Talk to Me* to give you that chance.

Please take the hope and lessons with you as you create your own loving garden. The lessons here will help you plant your flowers and pull your weeds. As you practice and learn, your garden will prosper. We also suggest that you take a look at the recommended reading list for more information.

Barrier 5. Depression or other mental conditions:

Depression is very common today and, fortunately, can be effectively treated in most cases. A depressed person can find life very difficult. These matters should be addressed by professionals. Some of the symptoms of depression may include the following: persistent sadness, feelings of hopelessness, pessimism, loss of interest in activities you once enjoyed, restlessness, decreased energy, thoughts of suicide, insomnia, oversleeping, difficulty making decisions and irritability. If you experience these symptoms, please talk to your doctor.

Timeliness

Time is fleeting and what you say or leave unsaid may live with you forever. Too many times you risk missing that one chance to say something important. For some couples, a missed chance may mean a moment or a lifetime of regret. On the other hand, when you take the opportunity to say "I love you" the goodness lives on. Words that are spoken in time are nurturing while those that aren't can create problems.

There may never be a perfect time to talk to your partner about something they might want to avoid but some times are certainly better than others. It helps to be considerate of your partner's daily routine. You may find, for example, that the time just before and after work are not good times to talk because he/she has so much on their mind. They won't feel ambushed if you pick a less stressful time such as after a meal or after their favorite television show.

If no time seems right or there has been a reluctance to talk, try making an appointment. You might say, for example, "I know you have a lot going on and I would like to discuss our weekend plans with you for about fifteen minutes. Would today after supper or tomorrow night before supper be better for you?" In this example you have picked a relatively safe topic to discuss and have offered a choice of brief times to make it easier for them to accept.

When you practice this approach over a period of time, you both will become more comfortable with making and keeping appointments. You will be able to work up to the more difficult topics on your list. You will build trust and confidence when you are clear and precise and you stay on one during the appointment, and use the guidelines for positive communication. Even when a subject is critical and you feel you must discuss it right away, it helps to offer a little time to prepare. For example, "Honey, I'm upset about our budget. I'd appreciate it if you would help me work through this tonight. Would you rather do it right now or in a half hour?" You communicated the topic, how you feel about it and asked for help in a straightforward and non-threatening way. Your chance of success is much higher than saying something like "You've spent too much money again and I want you to tell me what you're going to do about it right now. You're so selfish." Which approach would you prefer to use?

Make time to talk. You may find this is easier if you change your setting to reduce distractions or tension builders. Go out for a walk or take a ride in the car. Have some ice-cream or a cup of coffee. If you stay home, wait for the children to go to sleep, turn off the TV and unplug the phone. Try a little soft music in the background, relax, and take time to listen to each other.

Repression

Sometimes it may seem that there is not a good time to talk about some difficult subjects or feelings and you hold them in; repress them. Repressed feelings and frustrations may start to build up to the point where they explode. When feelings explode in the form of tirades, fights or hysterical breakdowns, it's almost impossible for the other partner to react in a positive way. It's human nature for the other partner to react with the same level of emotion. Don't believe the old wives' tale that it's good to fight to get the anger out on the table. **Anger only serves to create more anger.** It is like weeds going to seed and choking the garden.

If you are currently feeling a lot of frustration that has built up over time because you have held your feelings in, you may want to work on that frustration before you make it the primary topic to talk about with your partner. Pick a time when you both are more confident and calm. When you do make an appointment be sure to talk about how *you* feel using *"I"* statements and the guidelines.

Your feelings are as important as our partner's. Your relationship will benefit from clear and timely discussions when you follow the guidelines. You can build and maintain trust by encouraging each other to talk about things at the right time. Even the truth can seem like a lie when it is told too late or in too little detail. **Be honest, timely and kind and you will have a better chance of a win - win outcome when you are discussing problems.**

The Intimacy Trap: Barriers to Intimacy -- Overcome

Intimacy comes through communication: your words, your facial expressions and your touch become the fabric of your lives. These are the ways you communicate. Intimacy means sharing your feelings. You marry for the intimacy of the relationship. You hope the relationship will fill that empty part within you that you call loneliness and fulfill your need to be loved for who you are. That search, however, can become a trap that leaves you alone and unable to communicate. Intimacy becomes the focus of your relationship through courtship and into the first year or so of marriage. Then you may begin to wonder where your sense of self has gone. The passion of romance has faded, life has set in and you now face a number of barriers to intimacy and communication. Let's try to understand the intimacy trap so you can avoid it or work through it. You must create your own new intimate relationship independent of your parents and other prior relationships.

Here are six guidelines that will help you and your partner to work toward and achieve the intimacy you desire in your relationship.

1. *Fear of intimacy:*

How, you ask, can you fear intimacy or be reluctant to be intimate when that's what you seek so intently? The answer is simple - you are taught. You were taught from childhood that how others love and respect you depends on what *you do and accomplish.* You became a performer on stage anxious for reward and fearful of failure. Much of the love and recognition that you received was conditional upon that performance. You learned a need for and a fear of performance. This makes it difficult to get close to anyone for fear of judgment. You're driven by expectations that threaten your adequacy and personal self-worth. While romantic passion dominates the relationship and the communication, your fears are set aside. As passion fades, you return to your old relationships and activities in search of intimacy where judgment is less likely to be found. It's easier to be with friends, shop, go to the movies, read, surf the Web, play video games or to enjoy other stimulation rather than risk the possibility of judgment in an intimate conversation with your partner. This is especially true when you and/or your partner have become critical of each other. Criticism and arguments are intimate but not comfortable or positive for your relationship. We have counseled many couples who are intimate only when they are angry and unkind with each other. These relationships are out of balance.

Two of the ways to overcome a fear of intimacy are understanding and patience.

- Understand that fear may be playing a role in your relationship. Use the *Talk to Me* methods to help both you and your partner get a better view of what the situation is. You can use that understanding to help build a communication link between the two of you. Also understand that men generally tend to be intimate in ways that are different than women. Men like to just be together and do things with their partner while the women may want to talk about feelings and emotions with their mate.

- Be patient by understanding that change takes time. You can change yourself and your partner can change him/herself. As you build your communication, you will build an intimate connection and find a balance.

2. *Fear of conflict:*

Which is true: 1) A good relationship is one that has little to no conflict or 2) A good relationship has conflict? Most people believe that the first statement is true. You've been taught to avoid conflict and that conflict ruins relationships. This, however, creates a problem. **There cannot be intimacy without conflict.** We are not saying that conflict is fighting. We're not saying that fighting is discord. We are saying that conflict is any difference between two individuals in a relationship. You must have at least some level of conflict to have intimacy. You must be individuals to love. True love that's brought to the relationship comes from both of you as individuals. As individuals you have differences that will lead to conflict. Do not give up your identities when you enter a relationship. If you do that, you are bound to fail.

Relationships take strength from two individuals with differences coming together as one, yet remaining two.

How you handle differences and/or conflict determines the success or failure of the relationship.

If you communicate in a positive way, you have the opportunity to accommodate that difference in a way that builds intimacy and love. Catherine and I have, unfortunately, seen many relationships where the only intimacy that exists is in the form of abusive and destructive behavior. If you find yourself in an abusive relationship, please take action to stop it or leave.

It may be hard to remove yourself, but remember that there's more likelihood of success when both parties are in a physically and emotionally **safe place**.

3. *Misunderstanding intimacy:*

Even if you're unafraid of intimacy, you may not know how to be intimate. You may not know how to talk about yourself and your relationship because you've never been taught. You've been taught, quite often in fact, that you must not talk about yourself. It's too vain. Men, in particular, are taught to hide and control their feelings and emotions. The stoic tough guy image is portrayed in everything from advertisements to the movies. Even in school, especially sports, you are taught to "tough it out." Women, on the other hand, are more likely to have closer relationships with friends. They are more accustomed to talking about their feelings. These discussions, however, aren't always the ideal model for a married couple to follow. The roles and expectations are different for a married or otherwise committed couple.

You learned how to date from your equally young and confused friends, and were expected to present a "good image." Now in marriage you have to practice and work for an understanding of how to be intimate. You'll need to practice talking about important and difficult subjects with someone you love and are still getting to know.

Understand that neither of you may yet know how to be intimate or how to become intimate. A good place to start is with a discussion about the subject of intimacy. Use a statement like, "We haven't discussed how we will handle the important and sometimes difficult things we will face together in life. I think it would be a good idea if we talk about that. What do you think?" Or, "It will be good for our relationship when we create our own rules and guidelines for handling our disagreements."

4. *Exhaustion:*

You may find it exhausting to maintain the excitement of passion once the hormones and the newness have worn off. The wedding is no longer the focus and the mundane details of trying to live take over. The return to normalcy makes the relationship appear to be abnormal and cold. You might ask, "Why are we talking about bills when we used to talk about each other?" while you're thinking, "Don't you love me any more?" Normalcy includes the exhausting pressures of work, children, disappointments, in-law's, parents and expectations. You probably find it tiring at times to keep up with work, family and everything else. There must be times when it seems overwhelming and you just don't want anymore pressure, especially from your partner. At times like this you or your partner may tend to withdraw from being intimate or, worse, react with a short temper or inconsiderate behavior.

There are ways to recover. One way is for one of you to call a time-out, explaining that you're exhausted, that it's not your partner's fault and ask for help. We also recommend that you use the Couple's Fair Exchange Process, especially at times like this. The Process serves to validate your partner, while you are working toward understanding. Even if only one of you uses the Process and Guidelines for loving communication, you will create a better situation. This will help you get started with more positive changes.

5. *Self:*

You need to be yourself. Your highest priority in life should be yourself. Each of you should work on being individuals. You might forget this for a while in passion and place it second in favor of your relationship. But sooner or later you're likely to wake up and wonder where *you* are.

The best thing to do is to agree with your partner that you each need to come first as individuals and the relationship is a very close second. The happier you each are as individuals, the greater chance you have of having a loving and successful relationship. Please talk about this and encourage each other to have your own time and space to do things for yourself. It may take some adjustment to reach a balance. Be understanding of each other and work to preserve important relationships with family and friends. In the "Loving Garden" chapter you saw how important it was for Peter to continue to play ball with the team. It was also important for Anne to understand as well. You, like Anne and Peter, can create that balance. Become actively supportive of each other's career goals and personal objectives.

As your communication improves so will your ability to trust yourself and each other to do the right things. True love supports growth.

It may not, for example, be appropriate to go out partying a lot with old friends unless your partner is with you and you are enjoying the time together. Some adjustments in lifestyle should be made. The more you are able to understand each other's concerns and feelings, the stronger the relationship can become.

6. *Feelings:*

Feelings go far beyond the words that you think and say. They define much of who you are and how you experience life. If you don't understand your own feelings you cannot share them well. If you cannot share your feelings, you may feel frustrated or alone. Quite often people choose not to share their feelings for fear of hurting their partner and the relationship. This creates tension and a feeling of frustration that can be hard to deal with. You may find yourself in a relationship where you cannot have the loving understanding and comfort from your partner that you desire.

There are different ways you can experience your feelings. You can ignore them until they build up and boil over to an extreme, like anger or depression. You can react to them and let your feelings dictate how you will feel or behave at any moment. Or, you can choose to respond to your feelings in ways that are most appropriate to the moment. While any of these experiences are expected at one time or another, the most effective way to accommodate your feelings most of the time is to do so by choice.

Being able to make a choice about how you will respond or act in a particular situation allows you to use your communication skills in a positive way.

You may choose, for example, to let your partner know that you are feeling a particular way about something they are doing before it becomes a big issue with you. Doing this gives you the chance to talk about it while your emotions are still calm and you haven't built up resentment. As you both work through your feelings using the Guidelines and the Couple's Fair Exchange Process, you will learn how to be more understanding of both your own and your partner's feelings. It is important to do this on a regular basis.

You each have opinions and feelings about the way you should live. The better you understand what you share and what you disagree on, the better chance you have to create a positive, stable, loving relationship.

SUMMARY AND CONCLUSION:

Work on changing yourself in a positive way. You are responsible for your thoughts, words and deeds. You can develop understanding, kindness, honesty and respect in your communication and relationship.

You can overcome the barriers and blocks to intimate communication.

Here are 12 ways to succeed:

1. Make time to talk or just be there for each other. Be someone to lean on as a comfort to your partner.

2. Use the examples and recommendations in this book as an opportunity to learn. Follow the Couple's Fair Exchange Process and Guidelines.

3. Change your own behaviors first. Be a good example.

4. Take one small step at a time.

5. Build confidence in your skills by practicing them with others as well as your partner. Try them at work and with your friends.

6. Enlist your partner as an ally and teammate.

7. When your partner is ready, have them read along with you and share your evaluations and findings as you go.

8. If a technique or skill doesn't work for you adjust it or use something else.

9. Set positive objectives for yourself and your relationship and work toward them.

10. Keep up your faith in your ability to succeed.

11. Remember that "love" is a verb and you must take action to love.

12. Adopt and nourish a positive approach to life. Make positive affirmations every day.

The lessons of *Talk to Me* are our gift to you. Catherine and I have chosen to live our lives and create our own positive, loving communication based on these lessons. We hope that you too will choose to take a positive way for your life and relationships.

When you and your partner communicate well, your life and love will prosper. You will wake up each day with an ever-changing and growing love.

You will be alive and so will your love -- every new day. You and your lover will say "talk to me," and you will. You will talk to each other and create your own positive, loving communication one word at a time. Enjoy your growing, loving garden.

The Positive Way™

Resources & Recommended Reading List

<u>Adult Children As Husbands, Wives and Lovers</u> by Steven Farmer (This book provides solutions and creative ways to be with your partner and teaches Adult children how to become Adult Adults.)

<u>Couple's Guide to Communication</u> by John Gottman, Cliff Notarius, Jonni Gonso, Howard Markman (This book is excellent for teaching couples positive communication.)

<u>Creating Closer Families</u> *Principles of Positive Family Interaction* by William G. Dyer (This book is great for teaching families how to interact, especially between parent and child.)

<u>Creating Love</u> by John Bradshaw (This book teaches how to create more love in our lives.)

<u>Fighting for Your Marriage</u> by Howard Markman, Scott Stanley, & Susan Blumberg (This is an excellent book on how to prevent divorce and enhance relationships. Highly recommended.)

<u>Getting to the Heart of the Matter</u> by Dr. Paul Coleman (This book teaches couple how to resolve ongoing conflicts.)

<u>Getting the Love You Want</u> by Harville Hendrix (This is a guide for couples to discover their inner child and create a new relationship.)

<u>Home Coming: Reclaiming and Championing Your Inner Child</u> by John Bradshaw (This book or audio tape will help you to discover your inner child and learn how it affects you and your life today.)

<u>Light Her Fire</u> by Ellen Kreidman (This book teaches men how to treat the women in their lives and how to rekindle romance.)

<u>Light His Fire</u> by Ellen Kreidman (This book teaches women how to treat the men in their lives and how to rekindle romance.)

<u>Listening</u> by Matthew McKay & Patrick Fanning (This book teaches easy to learn listening skills.)

<u>Living the Seven Habits</u> by Stephen R. Covey (This book discusses the role of principles and values in life and how to honor those principles.)

<u>Men Are from Mars, Women Are from Venus</u> by John Gray (This book explores the differences in men and women and how to work with those differences.)

<u>Please Understand Me: Character & Temperament Types</u> by David Keirsey & Marilyn Bates (Contains personality profiles that you can take along, with detailed explanations of personality types.)

<u>Real Moments for Lovers</u> by Barbara De Angelis (This book shows couples how to find meaning in every moment and the joy of being in love.)

<u>The Game of Life & How to Play It</u> by Florence Scovel Shinn (This book tells how to get all the things we want in life by choosing the correct thoughts, words and deeds, along with using affirmations. Highly recommended.)

The Art of Loving by Erich Fromm (This book defines love, gives detail on all types of love, teaches what the differences are and reveals how to practice the art of loving.)

Why Marriages Succeed or Fail by John Gottman (This book gets to the real issues and problems couples face and gives solutions to the problems. Highly recommended.)

"Yes" or "No" The Guide to Better Decisions by Spencer Johnson (This is a guide for how to make better decisions in all areas of life.)

The Positive Way™

We invite you to call or write for information about seminars in your area and other *Positive Way* publications. Popular *Positive Way* relationship seminars include the following.

How to Create Positive Loving Communication

Based on the book, *Talk to Me: How to Create Positive Loving Communication*, this seminar teaches how to develop effective communication in relationships. Practical demonstrations show what really works even when there's conflict. Learn how to create love one word at a time.

How to Attract Your Ideal Mate

You will be more confident and effective in your search for companionship and love when you learn how to identify, find, attract and love your *ideal* mate. Learn the practical aspects of love and relationships and the do's and don'ts of attracting people. This is a very exciting opportunity to discover what really matters in love and relationships. Discover how to find love for a lifetime.

The Art of Loving Relationships - Creating Love

This rewarding seminar is designed for anyone in search of creating positive loving relationships. You will be more at peace with your self and your relationships when you learn what really matters in love. Discover how to practice the art of loving which will rekindle romance for long term love.

The Joy & Power of Positive Self-esteem

This seminar will help you create inner joy and personal power. Learn how to develop and create self-love and a positive self image even when you don't feel it's possible. Your relationship with yourself and others will be more enjoyable when you learn how to stop the inner critic and replace it with a positive, mentoring voice.

Private Consultations

Catherine and Steven Martin are available for individual private consultations on relationship concerns in general, communicating techniques, problem-solving methods for relationships and self-esteem development. Corporate consultations and training are available by arrangement.

Need an Inspiring and Informative Speaker?

Catherine and Steven Martin are accomplished and dynamic public speakers who would be pleased to present an educational and inspirational message to your audience. Topics include highlights of the key teachings from their seminars as well as other important issues relating to individual and relationship enhancement. Please contact them to arrange a presentation.

The Positive Way, 123 E. Pinelake Drive
Williamsville, NY 14221
phone 716-639-0225 • 800-664-4773
fax 716-636-1894